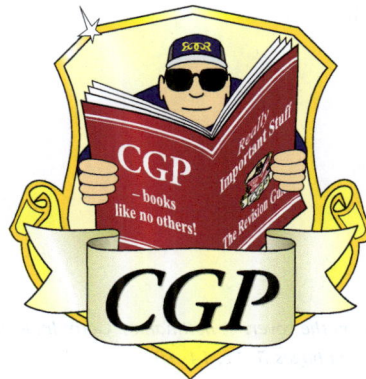

GCSE History is always topical with CGP...

If you're studying "Conflict and Tension between East and West, 1945–1972" for AQA GCSE History, this CGP Topic Guide will give your grades a lift-off like Sputnik.

It's packed with crystal-clear notes, plenty of helpful activities, sample answers, exam tips, exam-style questions and more. It's absolutely Khrushchev! Sorry, *crucial*.

How to access your free Online Edition

This book includes a free Online Edition to read on your PC, Mac or tablet.
To access it, just go to **cgpbooks.co.uk/extras** and enter this code...

3491 1909 9677 6093

By the way, this code only works for one person. If somebody else has used this book before you, they might have already claimed the Online Edition.

CGP — still the best! ☺

Our sole aim here at CGP is to produce the highest quality books — carefully written, immaculately presented and dangerously close to being funny.

Then we work our socks off to get them out to you — at the cheapest possible prices.

Published by CGP

Editors:
Andy Cashmore, Robbie Driscoll, Alex Fairer, Sophie Herring and Katya Parkes.

With thanks to Emma Cleasby, Holly Robinson and Helen Tanner for the proofreading.
With thanks to Emily Smith for the copyright research.

Acknowledgements:

With thanks to Getty Images for permission to use the image on the cover: © Bettmann / Getty Images.

With thanks to Rex Features for permission to use the images on pages 5, 11, 14, 19.

With thanks to Mary Evans for permission to use the images on pages 8, 32, 36, 44.

With thanks to TopFoto for permission to use the image on page 13.

Extract from a speech by Emanuel Shinwell on page 14 © Parliamentary Copyright. Contains Parliamentary information licensed under the Open Parliament Licence v3.0 https://www.parliament.uk/site-information/copyright-parliament/open-parliament-licence/.

With thanks to Look and Learn for permission to use the images on pages 16 and 30.

Extract from a statement given by President Truman following the dropping of the atom bomb on Hiroshima used on page 16, extract from NSC-68 used on page 19 and extract from a speech given by Averell Harriman used on page 25 from the Harry S. Truman Presidential Library and Museum.

With thanks to Alamy for permission to use the images on pages 17 and 24.

Image used on page 25: 'Uncle Sam' forcing the Western European nations to sign the North Atlantic Treaty on 4th April 1949, Russian caricature from 'Krokodil' magazine, 1949 (colour litho), Russian School, (20th century) / Private Collection / Archives Charmet / Bridgeman Images.

With thanks to Getty Images for permission to use the image on page 26.

Image used on page 33: National Archives (photo no. 6948996).

Extract from John F. Kennedy's 'Ich bin ein Berliner' speech used on page 37 from the John F. Kennedy Presidential Library and Museum.

Extract from a speech by John F. Kennedy about Cuba used on page 41 from the National Security Archive.

Image used on page 43: © The Times / News Licensing.

Extract used on page 45 from The Brezhnev Doctrine, 1968 from 'Pravda, September 25, 1968'; translated by Novosti, Soviet press agency

Image used on page 45: Marchers demonstrate outside the Soviet Trade Exhibition in Earls Court in protest of the Soviet lead invasion of Czechoslovakia, 22nd August 1968 (b/w photo) / London, UK / © Mirrorpix / Bridgeman Images.

Image used on page 50 from Red Primer for Children and Diplomats by Victor Vashi (1967).

Image used on page 50: © DACS 2019. Cartoon portraying the Soviet Union making a firm response to American attempts to overthrow the Communist regime in Cuba, 1961 (litho), Bidstrup, Herluf (1912-1988) / Private Collection / Look and Learn / Elgar Collection / Bridgeman Images.

Extract from a letter written by Nikita Khrushchev to John F. Kennedy used on page 51 from the U.S. State Department.

Every effort has been made to locate copyright holders and obtain permission to reproduce sources.
For those sources where it has been difficult to trace the copyright holder of the work, we would be grateful
for information. If any copyright holder would like us to make an amendment to the acknowledgements,
please notify us and we will gladly update the book at the next reprint. Thank you.

Contents

Exam Skills

The Origins of the Cold War

The Development of the Cold War

Transformation of the Cold War

Exam Hints and Tips

GCSE AQA History is made up of two papers. The papers test certain skills and each one covers different topics. This page gives you more information about each exam so you'll know what to expect.

You will take Two Papers altogether

It's really important that you make sure you know which topics you're studying for each paper.

Paper 1 covers the Period Study and the Wider World Depth Study

Paper 1 is 2 hours long. It's worth 84 marks — 50% of your GCSE. This paper will be divided into two sections:
- Section A: Period Study.
- Section B: Wider World Depth Study.

This book covers the Wider World Depth Study Conflict and Tension between East and West, 1945-1972.

Paper 2 covers the Thematic Study and the British Depth Study

Paper 2 is 2 hours long. It's worth 84 marks — 50% of your GCSE. This paper will be divided into two sections:
- Section A: Thematic Study.
- Section B: British Depth Study. This also includes a question on the Historic Environment.

Depth Studies are about knowing a Short Period in Detail

1) The depth studies cover a short period of history (less than 100 years) in detail. They focus on understanding how the main features and events of the period affected one another.

2) You'll need to have a detailed knowledge of the period — this means knowing the main developments and important events that took place. It also means understanding how important features of the Cold War period (e.g. political, social, economic and military issues) helped to shape events.

3) You should know the causes and consequences of the main events really well.

Wider World Depth Studies include questions about Sources

1) Sources are pieces of evidence from the period you're studying — such as a newspaper cartoon criticising the USSR's invasion of Hungary or an extract from a speech made by Leonid Brezhnev.

2) A source may also be someone's reflections on an issue or event they experienced, which was written or recorded after it took place. For example, a source could be an interview with someone who lived in Berlin when the Berlin Wall was built, carried out after the end of the Cold War.

3) Historians use sources to find out about and make sense of the past. They have to choose sources carefully to make sure they're useful for the specific question they are trying to answer.

4) Once they find a useful source, they use it to arrive at conclusions about the topic they're studying — this is called making inferences.

5) For the Wider World Depth Study, you'll be asked to evaluate the content and usefulness of different sources (see p.5).

Exam Hints and Tips

Remember these Tips for Approaching the Questions

Stay focused on the question

- Read the questions <u>carefully</u>. Underline the <u>key words</u> in each question so you know exactly what you need to do.
- Make sure that you <u>directly answer the question</u>. Don't just chuck in everything you know about the Cold War period.
- You've got to be <u>relevant</u> and <u>accurate</u> — make sure you include <u>precise details</u> in your answers.
- It might help to try to write the <u>first sentence</u> of every <u>paragraph</u> in a way that <u>addresses</u> the question, e.g. "Another reason why Cold War tensions increased in the 1960s was..."

> For example, you should include the <u>dates</u> of important events in the history of the Cold War and the <u>names</u> of the people who were involved.

Plan your essay answers

- You <u>don't</u> need to plan answers to the <u>shorter questions</u> in the exam.
- For <u>longer essay questions</u>, it's very important to make a <u>quick plan</u> before you start writing. This will help to make your answer <u>organised</u> and <u>well structured</u>, with each point <u>leading clearly</u> to your <u>conclusion</u>.
- Look at the <u>key words</u> in the question. Scribble a <u>quick plan</u> of your <u>main points</u> — <u>cross through this neatly</u> at the end, so it's obvious it shouldn't be marked.

Organise your Time in the exam

1) Always double-check that you know <u>how much time</u> you have for each paper.
2) <u>Learn the rule</u> — the <u>more marks</u> a question is worth, the <u>longer</u> your answer should be. The number of marks available for each question is clearly shown in the exam paper.
3) Don't get carried away writing loads for a question that's only worth four marks — you need to <u>leave time</u> for the higher mark questions.
4) Try to leave a few minutes at the <u>end</u> of the exam to go back and <u>read over</u> your answers.

Always use a Clear Writing Style

1) Try to use <u>clear handwriting</u> — and pay attention to <u>spelling</u>, <u>grammar</u> and <u>punctuation</u>. In the <u>16-mark question</u>, there are an <u>extra 4 marks</u> available for SPaG.
2) If you make a mistake, miss out a word or need to add extra information to a point, make your changes <u>neatly</u>. Check that the examiner will still be able to <u>easily read</u> and <u>understand</u> your answer.
3) Remember to start a <u>new paragraph</u> for each new point you want to discuss.
4) A brief <u>introduction</u> and <u>conclusion</u> will help to give <u>structure</u> to your essay answers and make sure you stay <u>focused</u> on the <u>question</u>.

EXAM TIP

Learn this page and make exam stress history...

Jotting down a quick plan of the different points you're going to make before you start writing can really help you to make sure your answer is clearly written and has a nice logical structure.

Skills for the Wider World Depth Study

These two pages will give you some advice on how to approach the Wider World Depth Study, as well as how to find your way around this book. Activity types are colour-coded to help you find what you need.

The Wider World Depth Study tests Three different Skills

1) Throughout the Wider World Depth Study, you'll be expected to show your knowledge and understanding of the topic, as well as your ability to apply historical concepts, such as cause and consequence.

2) For questions which ask you to analyse sources you'll also need to use more specific skills.

3) The activities in this book will help you to practise all the different skills you'll need for the Wider World Depth Study exam.

Knowledge and Understanding

1) Although you'll be given sources in the exam, you'll still need to use your own knowledge and understanding of the topic to back up your answers.

2) It's important that you use accurate and relevant information to support your ideas, especially when you're answering questions 3 and 4.

> The Knowledge and Understanding activities in this book will help you to revise key features and events from the period — what was happening, when it was happening, who was involved and all the other important details.

Thinking Historically

1) As well as knowing what happened when, you also need to use historical concepts like cause and consequence to analyse key events and developments.

2) Question 3 will ask you to write a narrative account of developments that took place during the Cold War. It will focus on the causes and/or consequences of the developments.

3) When you're answering this question, don't just describe what happened — analyse every event that you write about. Think about the impact that it had and explain how different events were related.

4) Question 4 will give you a statement about the Cold War period and ask you how far you agree with it.

5) For this question, decide your opinion before you start writing and state it clearly at the beginning and end of your answer. Don't forget to include different sides of the argument, even if you don't agree with them — this shows you've considered all of the evidence.

> Give an account of how events in Cuba increased tension between the superpowers from 1959 to 1962. [8 marks]

> 'The USSR's actions were the main reason for Cold War tensions in Asia in the 1950s'. Explain how far you agree with this statement. [16 marks]

> The Thinking Historically activities in this book will help you to practise using historical concepts to analyse different parts of the topic.

> For questions like this in the exam, 4 extra marks will be available for spelling, punctuation, grammar and using specialist terms.

Skills for the Wider World Depth Study

Source Analysis

In the exam, you'll need to answer two different source-based questions:

1) Question 1 will ask you to evaluate what a visual or written source is saying.

2) When answering this question, it's important that you don't just describe what you can see or read in the source. You need to read between the lines and use your own knowledge to draw conclusions about what the source is suggesting.

3) Question 2 involves two more sources. You'll have to explain how useful each source is for studying a particular aspect of the Cold War.

4) For each source, you should think about:
   - The date — when the source was produced
   - The author — who produced it
   - The purpose — why it might have been produced
   - The content — what the source says or shows

5) In your answer, you need to explain how these factors affect the usefulness of the source for studying the topic given in the question.

> How can you tell that Source A supports the USA? Use Source A and your own knowledge to explain your answer. [4 marks]

> Look at Source B and Source C. How useful would these sources be to a historian studying the expansion of Soviet communism between 1945 and 1949? Use both sources and your own knowledge to explain your answer. [12 marks]

> The content of this cartoon is useful because it shows a noose reaching from the USSR and surrounding Czechoslovakia. This makes it look as though Czechoslovakia is about to be strangled and killed, which suggests that the expansion of Soviet communism to Czechoslovakia would have terrible consequences for the country. Political cartoons often reflect public attitudes, so this cartoon is useful because it suggests that the American public viewed the expansion of Soviet communism between 1945 and 1949 as threatening and harmful.

6) You will be given both written and visual sources in the exam, but you should handle them both in the same way.

> The Source Analysis activities in this book will help you to practise understanding sources, evaluating what they are saying and analysing their usefulness.

An American cartoon published in 1947. The cartoon shows a noose around Czechoslovakia. The buildings in the background represent the USSR.

EXAM TIP

Modern history — remembering what you did yesterday...

Dealing with sources might seem a bit tricky at first, but don't worry — this book is crammed with useful questions and activities to help you practise all of the skills that you'll need.

The Origins of the Cold War

The End of the Second World War

The alliance of the 'big three' from World War Two (Britain, the USA and the USSR) was known as the Grand Alliance. Their desire to defeat Nazi Germany united them, but as the war ended, tensions emerged.

The USA and the USSR had very Different Ideologies

1) The USA and the USSR were allies during the Second World War, but they had very different beliefs:

> The USA was capitalist. It had a democratically elected government, and its economy was based on private ownership of property, free competition and forces of supply and demand. Americans believed in personal rights and freedoms, such as freedom of speech.

> The USSR was communist. It was a single-party state, and its economy was controlled by the government, with no private ownership of property. The state decided what rights its citizens had, and it could also take these rights away. Freedom of speech was restricted.

2) Communism aimed at world revolution, so it was seen by Americans as a danger to their democracy and freedoms. However, the communists also feared worldwide American influence — they believed that capitalism led to the exploitation of workers and the unfair distribution of wealth.

The 'Big Three' discussed Europe's Future at Yalta

1) In February 1945, the Grand Alliance held a conference at Yalta in the Soviet Union. By this time the Allies were confident of winning the war, so talks focused on how Germany should be dealt with after it was defeated.

> The USSR (Union of Soviet Socialist Republics) was also known as the Soviet Union.

2) The three leaders attended the conference with different aims:

> The leader of the Soviet Union, Joseph Stalin, wanted to gain influence over Eastern European countries — he feared attacks from the West and thought that these countries would help protect the USSR.

> US president Franklin D. Roosevelt wanted to create the United Nations (UN). It would be a peacekeeping force and allow the US to step back from Europe. He wanted to co-operate with Stalin, partly to secure his support against Japan (p.8).

> British Prime Minister Winston Churchill aimed to preserve Britain's global power and limit the USSR's influence in Europe. He also wanted to ensure that Germany would be politically and economically stable, to avoid further unrest there.

3) Despite the leaders' different aims, talks seemed to go well at Yalta. Many key decisions were made:

- Eastern Europe would be the Soviet Union's 'sphere of influence'.
- Liberated Eastern European countries would hold free elections.
- Germany and Berlin would each be divided into four zones, and these would be shared between the 'big three' plus France.
- The United Nations would replace the failed League of Nations.

> Before Yalta, the Red Army (the USSR's army) had liberated Poland from Nazi rule, and a Soviet-friendly, communist government had been set up there. These actions concerned the West, so at Yalta, Stalin agreed to let non-communists join the government and to hold free elections.

Potsdam revealed the First Cracks in the Grand Alliance

1) After Germany surrendered in May 1945, the allied leaders met again at Potsdam over July and August.

2) Some things at Potsdam were different to Yalta. Roosevelt had died in April 1945, and Harry Truman was now US President. Britain also had a new leader — Clement Attlee replaced Churchill mid-conference.

3) Some agreements were finalised at Potsdam — the new boundaries of Poland were agreed, and it was confirmed that Germany and Berlin would be divided into zones and split between the Allies.

4) However, relations between the 'big three' became much more hostile at Potsdam:

- Britain and the US were alarmed by Stalin's actions in Poland — he was installing a government made up of only pro-communist members. Britain and the USA felt this went against the Yalta agreement.
- Truman was more suspicious of the USSR and less willing to compromise. He wanted to limit Soviet influence in Eastern Europe and to stop communism from spreading. Attlee was also concerned about Soviet expansion, but he seemed eager for the conference to be over.
- The Allies had differing views over Germany. They disagreed over the boundaries of their zones, and didn't decide if, or when, the zones could rejoin and form a country again. While Stalin wanted to keep Germany weak, Truman worried this would make Germany vulnerable to Soviet expansion.

The End of the Second World War

SKILLS PRACTICE

The Grand Alliance developed during the Second World War, but once the war was over there was little left to unite its members. Try these activities to make sure you know how and why the alliance fell apart.

Knowledge and Understanding

1) The USA was a capitalist country and the USSR was a communist country. Copy and complete the table below about the ideological differences between the two countries.

Country	Politics	Economy	Human rights
a) The USA			
b) The USSR			

2) Explain why the USA and the USSR disliked each other's ideologies.

3) Describe the aims of the following leaders at Yalta. Give as much detail as you can.

a) Joseph Stalin   b) Franklin D. Roosevelt   c) Winston Churchill

4) Copy and complete the mind map below by adding in the key agreements made at Yalta and Potsdam.

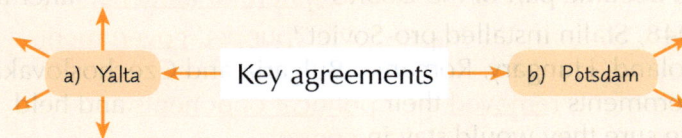

a) Yalta ← Key agreements → b) Potsdam

Thinking Historically

1) Copy and complete the diagram below by explaining the consequence of each event for the relationship between the USA and the USSR.

President Roosevelt dies. → a) Consequence

Stalin is installing a pro-communist government in Poland after Yalta. → b) Consequence

2) Explain how and why the relationship between the members of the Grand Alliance changed during 1945. Use your answer to question 1 above to help you.

'East' and 'West' had different perspectives...

EXAM TIP

Make sure you know how much time to spend on each question in the exam — if one question is worth twice as many marks as another, you should spend about twice as long answering it.

The Two Superpowers

The USSR and the USA emerged from the Second World War as the <u>two</u> biggest <u>powers</u> in the world. But they were very <u>suspicious</u> of one another, and began to interpret each other's actions as <u>threats</u>.

The USA kept its Atom Bomb a Secret

1) <u>Japan</u> was on Germany's side in the war, and <u>continued to fight</u> after Germany <u>surrendered</u> in May 1945. In August 1945, the USA dropped two <u>atom bombs</u> on Japan — <u>destroying</u> the cities of <u>Hiroshima</u> and <u>Nagasaki</u>.

2) The atom bombs meant that military help from the USSR <u>wasn't needed</u> to defeat Japan. President Truman also <u>refused</u> to allow the USSR to take part in the US <u>occupation</u> of Japan.

3) The USA had kept the exact nature of the atom bomb a <u>secret</u> from the USSR at <u>Potsdam</u> in July 1945 (although Stalin's spies had passed on many details).

4) For four years, the USA was the <u>only</u> country in the world with nuclear weapons. This <u>boosted</u> the <u>power</u> and <u>status</u> of the USA, and gave it an <u>advantage</u> over the USSR. Stalin saw the development of the atom bomb as an attempt to <u>intimidate</u> the USSR, and was angry that the USA had managed to <u>surpass</u> Soviet technology.

5) The atom bombs <u>increased the rivalry</u> between the USA and the USSR. The USSR sped up the development of its own atomic bomb, starting an <u>arms race</u> between the two countries (see p.22).

The atom bomb caused devastation in Hiroshima.

© Everett Collection / Mary Evans

This made Stalin more suspicious of the West, which increased <u>tensions</u> between the superpowers.

The USSR became Influential in Eastern Europe

1) At the end of the Second World War, the <u>Red Army</u> (p.6) occupied <u>Eastern Europe</u>. These countries would become part of the USSR's <u>sphere of influence</u> after the war.

2) Between 1945 and 1948, Stalin installed pro-Soviet '<u>puppet</u>' <u>governments</u> in countries such as Poland, Hungary, Romania, Bulgaria and Czechoslovakia. These communist governments <u>removed</u> their <u>political opponents</u> and held <u>fixed elections</u> to make sure they would stay in <u>control</u>.

The Red Army had <u>liberated</u> Eastern Europe from <u>Nazism</u>, and Stalin felt that the countries in this region should stay under <u>Soviet control</u>.

- For a while it seemed that <u>Czechoslovakia</u> might remain democratic. But when the Communist Party seemed likely to lose ground in the next election, it <u>seized power</u> in February 1948.

- When Germany was <u>divided</u> between the Allies at <u>Yalta</u>, the <u>USSR</u> was given <u>East Germany</u>. The USSR installed a <u>communist government</u> there too. Stalin told a group of German communists to join with the German <u>Social Democratic Party</u> (SPD) and form the <u>Socialist Unity Party of Germany</u> (SED). The communists then <u>removed</u> original members of the SPD and took control.

There was an 'Iron Curtain' between East and West

1) Increasing tensions between the USA and the USSR became known as the '<u>Cold War</u>'. There was no direct fighting — both sides were <u>afraid</u> of another war, especially after 1949, when the USSR had its own nuclear weapons (see p.22).

2) Countries in <u>Western Europe</u> tended to support the <u>USA</u>. Most countries in <u>Eastern Europe</u> were dominated by the <u>USSR</u>. In a famous speech in 1946, Winston Churchill warned there was an '<u>Iron Curtain</u>' dividing Europe.

— The Iron Curtain

Norway · Sweden · Finland · Denmark · Netherlands · Great Britain · Germany · Poland · USSR · Belgium · Czechoslovakia · France · Switz. · Austria · Hungary · Romania · Italy · Yugoslavia · Bulgaria · Albania · Turkey

Countries under the <u>influence</u> of the USSR became known as its '<u>satellite states</u>' (in pink).

Comment and Analysis

Churchill's '<u>Iron Curtain</u>' speech demonstrates the <u>breakdown</u> of the Grand Alliance — Britain and the USA now viewed the USSR as a <u>threat</u>, not an <u>ally</u>.

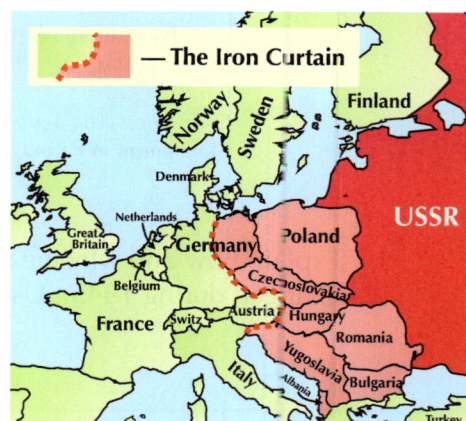

The Two Superpowers

These activities will help you understand how the USA and the USSR went from being allies to being enemies.

Knowledge and Understanding

1) Explain how the USA used its atom bombs in 1945.

2) After the Second World War, the USSR made several states, such as Czechoslovakia and East Germany, into its satellite states. Name four more of the USSR's satellite states.

3) Copy and complete the table below, explaining how each state became communist.

State	How it became communist
a) Czechoslovakia	
b) East Germany	

4) Write a definition of each of the following terms:

a) Cold War   b) Iron Curtain

Thinking Historically

1) Copy and complete the mind map below by explaining the reasons why the development of the atom bomb increased tension between the USA and the USSR. Include as much detail as possible.

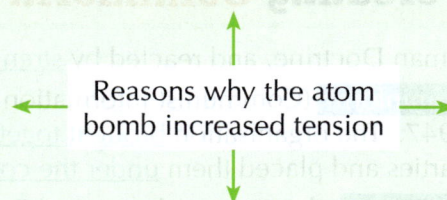

Reasons why the atom bomb increased tension

2) Explain why the USSR's actions in Eastern Europe from 1945 to 1948 increased tension between the USSR and the Western powers. Use information from page 6 to help you.

3) What does Churchill's 'Iron Curtain' speech show about relations between the West and the USSR after World War Two?

EXAM TIP

My two favourite superpowers — flying and invisibility...

It's important to understand that both countries believed that the other wanted to destroy them — so any steps that one side took to protect itself might be seen by the other side as an attack.

Mutual Suspicion

The Cold War was a period of international tension — with each side suspicious of the other.

Truman Acted to Contain the Communist Threat

1) President Truman was extremely worried that communism would spread to Western Europe. Many countries were undergoing economic hardships as a result of World War Two which Truman thought might make communism look more appealing.

2) Truman thought that if Western European countries became communist, capitalism and the USA's status as a global power would decline. The USA decided to intervene in Europe — the government introduced a policy of containment to try and stop the spread of communism.

The Truman Doctrine (announced March 1947)

- The USA pledged to support any nation threatened by a communist takeover. This support could be diplomatic, military or financial. For example, the USA gave $400 million of aid to Turkey and Greece to stop communism spreading.
- The USA believed that it was its duty to help those who were facing pressure from communist forces, and that intervention was the only way to maintain both world peace and American security.

Comment and Analysis

The USA had previously avoided becoming involved in European issues during peacetime. The scale of this containment policy shows how concerned they were about the spread of communism.

The Marshall Plan (announced June 1947)

- This promised $17 billion of aid to European countries to help rebuild their economies — the areas of Germany under Western occupation benefitted massively.
- Countries receiving aid were expected to co-operate with the USA and to import American goods.
- Stalin ordered all of his satellite states to reject the plan. The Soviets accused the USA of 'dollar imperialism' — using financial aid to gain power and influence in Europe. The USSR believed that America was trying to lure Eastern European states away from communism.

As well as containing communism, the US government argued that the Marshall Plan would help ease suffering in Europe. The plan would also create markets for US goods in Europe, which would benefit the US economy.

The USSR Reacted by creating Cominform

1) Stalin felt threatened by the Truman Doctrine, and reacted by strengthening and uniting his allies.

- Cominform (Communist Information Bureau) was set up in September 1947. The organisation brought together all European communist parties and placed them under the control of the USSR.
- Comecon (the Council for Mutual Economic Assistance) was established in January 1949. It placed industry and agriculture under state control and offered satellite states economic aid as an alternative to the Marshall Plan.

2) Stalin hoped this would encourage economic development in Eastern Europe and discourage trade with the West. It also appeased the countries that had been ordered to refuse Marshall aid.

Comment and Analysis

Marshall Plan aid ensured that a lot of Western Europe became allied with the USA. Stalin's retaliation — his creation of Cominform and, later, Comecon — strengthened his alliances in Eastern Europe.

Stalin wanted Complete Control over his 'Sphere Of Influence'

1) Stalin expected communist states in Eastern Europe to follow Soviet policies and ideas without question.

2) However, Yugoslavia challenged Soviet domination. It had freed itself from the Nazis without the Red Army, so owed less loyalty to the USSR. Yugoslavia was communist but more open to the West, and its leader, Tito, often refused to obey Stalin. This caused great tension between the two leaders.

3) Eventually, in June 1948, Stalin expelled Yugoslavia from Cominform and the country became an independent communist state. Yugoslavia later received economic aid from the USA.

Mutual Suspicion

Use these activities to test your understanding of how each side's fear of the other led to increasing tensions.

Knowledge and Understanding

1) Explain what each of the following policies were and why the USA introduced them:

   a) The Truman Doctrine
   b) The Marshall Plan

2) Explain how Stalin reacted to the Truman Doctrine and the Marshall Plan. Give as much detail as possible in your answer.

3) How was Yugoslavia different from the other countries in Eastern Europe in the 1940s?

Source Analysis

Source A

© Granger/Shutterstock

Source A is an American cartoon, published in 1947. It is called 'The Way Back'. The man is labelled 'Europe' and he is climbing a rope labelled 'Marshall Plan'. The area below represents communism.

Source B

... the imperialist* camp and its directing force, the United States of America, show a growing aggressive activity. This activity evolved at the same time in all spheres: in the sphere of military and strategic activities, economic expansion and ideological** warfare. The Truman-Marshall plan is only a farce***, a European branch of the general world plan of political expansion being realized**** by the United States of America in all parts of the world.

*those who believe powerful nations should control weaker ones
**relating to beliefs   ***joke   ****carried out

Source B is an extract from a statement about the creation of Cominform, made by communist parties from nine European countries. It was written on 4th October 1947.

1) Imagine you are using Source A for an investigation into attitudes towards the Marshall Plan. Explain how the features listed below affect its usefulness for your investigation.

   a) Where the source was produced
   b) When the source was produced
   c) Content of the source

2) How do the author, date and content of Source B affect its usefulness for the same investigation?

3) Why do you think the sources might be useful as a pair for investigating attitudes towards the Marshall Plan?

EXAM TIP

The Cold War was tense — but preferable to a hot one...

With so much happening in a short space of time, it's easy to get muddled. Thinking about how one event led to another can help you to keep track of what happened when.

The Berlin Crisis

Tension over the division of Germany had been building since the Potsdam Conference, and finally spilled over in the Berlin crisis in 1948. It resulted in an even larger rift between the two great powers.

In 1948 the USSR tried to take Control of Berlin...

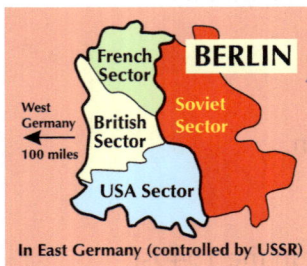

Map showing French Sector, BERLIN, British Sector, Soviet Sector, USA Sector, West Germany 100 miles. In East Germany (controlled by USSR)

1) Immediately after the war, occupied Germany was divided into four zones (see p.6). Berlin was in East Germany — the zone occupied by the USSR. Berlin was also split into four zones. The Soviet sector of the city was called East Berlin, while the French, British and US sectors formed West Berlin.

2) In 1947, the USA and Britain combined their zones to form 'Bizonia'. In 1948, the French added their zone too.

3) The new western zone had a single government, and in June 1948 introduced a new currency to help economic recovery.

4) This alarmed the USSR. Stalin did not want a unified western zone on his doorstep. West Berlin's strong capitalist economy embarrassed the USSR, and made communism look weak.

5) As a result, Stalin decided to blockade Berlin to try to force the capitalist powers to withdraw from West Berlin. In June 1948, he ordered that all road, rail and canal links between West Berlin and the outside world should be cut off.

6) The blockade meant that West Berlin faced shortages of food and other essential items, such as fuel, water and medicine. It also meant that travel to and from Berlin was severely restricted.

Comment and Analysis

Stalin wanted to force the West to withdraw from Berlin altogether. The Western powers believed that if this happened, the Soviet Union would be tempted to invade West Germany.

... but the West was Determined to keep its zones

1) The Western powers refused to give up West Berlin — retreating from the city would have given the Soviets the upper hand. They decided to bypass the blockade and fly supplies into West Berlin.

2) This became known as the Berlin Airlift and lasted for 318 days. By 1949, 8000 tons of supplies were being flown in every day. Exports were also flown out of West Berlin, which allowed trade to continue.

3) Tegel airport was built in West Berlin to accommodate the large volume of flights. It meant supplies could be delivered in even greater numbers.

4) Life was still tough in West Berlin during the Airlift. Food and electricity were rationed, and shortages of coal meant that many people struggled to heat their homes, an issue which became worse during winter.

The crisis Worsened Relations between East and West

1) It became clear that the West was determined not to withdraw from Berlin, so Stalin unwillingly lifted the blockade in May 1949. He had failed to bring the whole city under Soviet control.

2) The Berlin crisis gave America a huge propaganda victory over the USSR. Stalin was discredited and humiliated, while the USA seemed strong and committed to protecting freedom from Soviet aggression. The USA also earned the respect of many Germans, who now viewed the Americans as defenders and not just an occupying force.

The suffering caused by the blockade severely damaged the USSR's reputation in Europe.

Comment and Analysis

The Berlin crisis was the first major confrontation of the Cold War. It increased tensions between the USA and the USSR, and showed that the USA was dedicated to its policy of containment (see p.10). Berlin would remain a source of conflict between the two powers.

3) It seemed unlikely that the two powers would come to an agreement over Berlin — it was clear that Germany would remain divided. In 1949, two separate states were formed — West Germany (Federal Republic of Germany) and communist East Germany (German Democratic Republic).

During the Airlift, the Soviets hadn't dared to shoot at US planes — they knew that they couldn't compete if the USA responded with nuclear weapons. This weakness may have contributed to Stalin's desire to develop the atomic bomb.

The Berlin Crisis

There's a lot to learn on the previous page, so use these activities to check you really know your stuff.

Thinking Historically

1) Copy and complete the diagram below, explaining the effect that each event or development had.

| West Berlin develops a strong economy. | → | a) Effect on the USSR | → | Stalin decides to blockade West Berlin. | → | b) Effect on West Berlin |

2) Copy and complete the mind map below by adding the consequences of the Berlin crisis for each of the following:

a) US propaganda

d) The future of Germany ← **Consequences of the Berlin crisis** → b) The attitude of Germans to the USA

c) The USSR's reputation in Europe

Source Analysis

1) The source below is a British cartoon published on 14th July 1948 during the Berlin Airlift. The source is critical of the USSR. Explain how each of the highlighted details below shows this.

a) Birds are carrying bags of coal and food to West Berlin.

b) The birds are storks. Storks are associated with birth and bringing new life.

c) Stalin is watching the storks while holding a gun.

THE BIRD WATCHER

© Punch Cartoon Library / TopFoto

EXAM TIP

The West had made Stalin look weak...

Including specific names, dates and statistics in an answer shows that you know the topic well. Just make sure any details you use are relevant and help to explain the point you're making.

Worked Exam-Style Question

The sample answer below will give you an idea of how to analyse the usefulness of two sources.

Source A

A Hungarian poster published in February 1945. The man at the centre of the poster is Hitler.

Source B

We on this side are all for international co-operation; it has been our ideal for many long years. I am bound to say, however, that there is very little hope of promoting international co-operation... unless we can get unity among the three great Allies... If there is… suspicion among the three great Allies, what is the use of pretending to the small nations that we can offer them protection… but I want to say that the declarations of Yalta are a magnificent advance on anything that has gone before. I believe they have taken the first definite step towards an enduring peace.

An extract from a speech by Emanuel Shinwell, a British politician, about the Yalta Conference. It was made on 28th February 1945 — 17 days after the conference ended.

Look at Source A and Source B. How useful would these sources be to a historian studying the relationship between Britain, the USA and the USSR in 1945? Use both sources and your own knowledge to explain your answer. [12 marks]

> This **directly addresses** the question.

Source A is useful for studying the relationship between Britain, the USA and the USSR in 1945, because it shows that some people believed that the alliance which had emerged between these three nations during the war was strong. The source was published at a time when the Allies were confident of victory in the Second World War, and it portrays Britain, the USA and the Soviet Union working together to defeat Hitler and Nazism. This suggests that the three nations were united by a common goal and that their 'Grand Alliance' was important for military victory. Therefore, this source is useful because, as it was published in Hungary, it shows that some people in Eastern Europe saw the Grand Alliance as powerful and effective.

> When you're analysing a **visual source**, remember to **explain what it shows**.

> You need to refer to **both sources** in your answer.

Source B is useful because it shows that in 1945, it was already acknowledged that the Grand Alliance would need to co-operate to maintain its relationship. In the source, Shinwell seems to suggest that the Allies needed to focus on achieving 'unity' and avoiding feelings of

Worked Exam-Style Question

'suspicion' among themselves, which hints that the Grand Alliance might face difficulties working together. Indeed, the relationship between Britain, the USA and the USSR did face significant challenges. The USSR followed a communist ideology, which was completely opposed to capitalist Britain and America, and this caused the Soviets and the West to view each other with distrust. These tensions were already visible at the time of the Yalta Conference, with the West being concerned by Stalin's decision to install a communist government in Poland. Source B is useful therefore, because it reveals that in 1945, some political figures were aware of potential problems facing the Grand Alliance.

Use your own knowledge to support your argument.

Source B is also useful because it suggests that although the relationship between Britain, the USA and the USSR potentially faced difficulties, the relationship also had its strengths. Shinwell refers to the agreements made at the Yalta Conference as a 'magnificent advance', and the 'first definite step towards an enduring peace'. This suggests that Shinwell believed that the countries were capable of working well together. Indeed, Churchill, Roosevelt and Stalin had successfully reached agreements on key issues at Yalta, such as the division of Germany and the formation of the United Nations. This source is also useful because, when taken together with Source A, it shows that people in both Eastern and Western Europe believed that the Grand Alliance could work together effectively.

Refer to details from the sources to back up your points.

You could discuss how considering the sources together affects their usefulness.

Overall, Source B is more useful than Source A for studying the relationship between Britain, the USA and the USSR in 1945. Shinwell was a politician from an Allied nation, so his knowledge of the relationship between the members of the Grand Alliance is likely to be more accurate than that of an artist from Hungary. This superior knowledge is reflected in the content of the source. While Shinwell gives more detailed and specific information about the Grand Alliance in Source B, Source A gives a more simplistic and generalised view of the relationship, and this limits its usefulness.

This provides a clear judgement about which source is more useful.

This discusses the creators of both sources. It's important to discuss the origin of sources, such as who produced them, as this can affect their usefulness.

However, both sources have limitations. They were produced in the February of 1945, so they can't offer a complete view of the relationship between the three countries during that year. For instance, disagreements at the Potsdam Conference during July and August saw the relationship worsen significantly. Therefore, while Source B is more useful than Source A, neither source gives a full picture of the relationship between Britain, the USA and the USSR in 1945.

You could also comment on why the sources might be less useful to a historian.

Make sure you link your analysis back to the question.

Exam-Style Questions

Have a go at these exam-style questions to test your knowledge of the early stages of the Cold War.

Source A

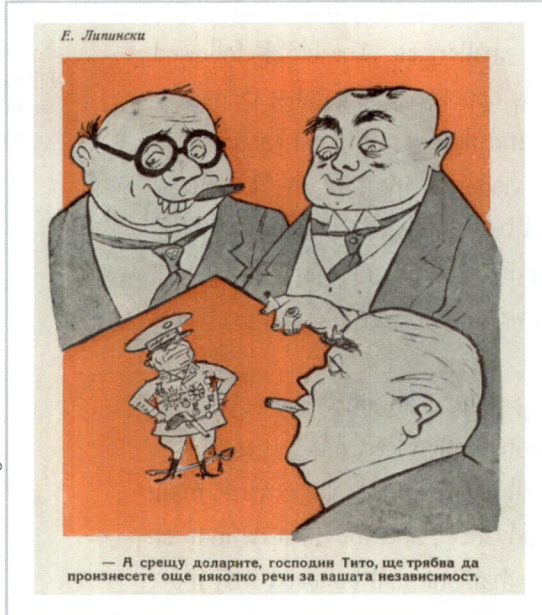

Е. Липински

— А срещу доларите, господин Тито, ще трябва да произнесете още няколко речи за вашата независимост.

© Look and Learn / Elgar Collection

A cartoon produced around 1950. The small figure is Tito, the leader of Yugoslavia. The three figures around him represent the West.

The text at the bottom of the cartoon can be translated as 'And now in exchange for the dollars — you have to hold a few speeches about your 'independence'.'

Source B

An extract from a statement made by President Truman on 6th August 1945 — sixteen hours after the USA dropped an atomic bomb on Hiroshima. He is discussing the significance of the bomb, and how the USA planned to handle its nuclear advantage.

> With this bomb we have now added a new and revolutionary increase in destruction to supplement* the growing power of our armed forces. In their present form these bombs are now in production and even more powerful forms are in development... But under present circumstances it is not intended to divulge** the technical processes of production or all the military applications, pending*** further examination of possible methods of protecting us and the rest of the world from the danger of sudden destruction. I shall recommend that the Congress of the United States**** consider promptly the establishment of an appropriate commission to control the production and use of atomic power within the United States. I shall give further consideration and make further recommendations to the Congress as to how atomic power can become a powerful and forceful influence towards the maintenance of world peace.

*strengthen   **reveal   ***until there has been

****the part of the US government responsible for making laws

Exam-Style Questions

Source C

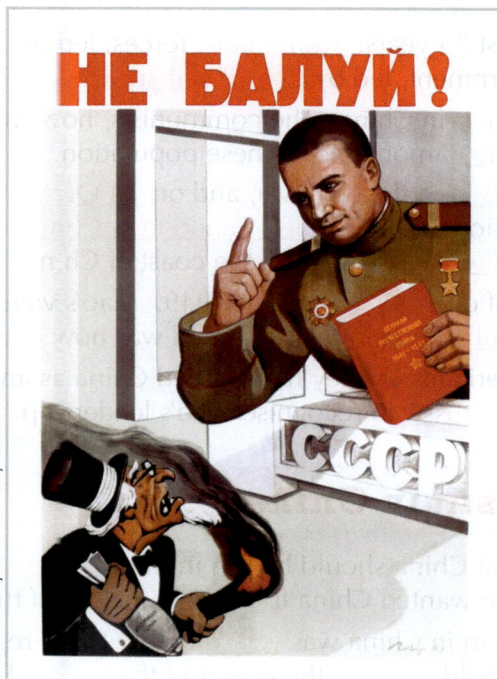

© World History Archive / Alamy Stock Photo

A poster produced by the Soviet Union in 1948.

The figure in the window represents the Soviet Union, and the figure holding the flaming torch represents the USA.

The text at the top can be translated as 'Do not fool around!'.

Exam-Style Questions

1) How can you tell that Source A is critical of the West?
   Use Source A and your own knowledge to explain your answer.   [4 marks]

2) Look at Source B and Source C. How useful would these sources be to a historian studying attitudes towards America's possession of the atom bomb?
   Use both sources and your own knowledge to explain your answer.   [12 marks]

3) Give an account of how the Berlin Crisis (1948-49) increased Cold War tensions.   [8 marks]

4) 'Stalin's desire to expand Soviet influence in Eastern Europe was the main reason for the development of the Cold War between 1945 and 1949.'

   Explain how far you agree with this statement.   [16 marks]

> For the 16-mark question in the exam, 4 extra marks will be available for spelling, punctuation, grammar and using specialist terminology.

The Development of the Cold War

The USSR and China

The superpowers had concentrated on events unfolding in Europe, but communism was also growing in Asia.

China became a Communist State in 1949

1) By 1949, China had been in a state of civil war for almost 25 years. Communist forces, led by Mao Tse-tung, challenged the country's Nationalist government, led by Chiang Kai-shek.

2) Chiang's government was corrupt, and it was losing support in China. The communists, however, wanted to modernise the country and had a large following among the Chinese population

> Mao's victory in China made it seem as though communism was becoming increasingly powerful — many Americans felt threatened by this.

3) Eventually the communists won the civil war, and on 1st October 1949, Mao announced the creation of the People's Republic of China. The Nationalists fled to Taiwan, an island off the coast of China.

4) China had a population of over 500 million in 1949. Mao's victory meant that the most heavily populated nation in the world was now communist.

5) China's 'fall' to communism was a massive shock to Americans — they had viewed China as an ally that shared American values. Truman's government refused to recognise Mao's leadership.

Stalin supported Mao and Communism in China

1) Mao admired Stalin's style of leadership and believed that China should be run in the same way as the Soviet Union. In June 1949, Mao had announced that he wanted China to become an ally of the USSR.

2) Stalin was more hesitant to embrace China — communism in China was very different to his regime in the Soviet Union, and he was also worried that China would threaten the power of the USSR. However, Stalin recognised Mao as the rightful leader of China and supported communism in the country.

3) In February 1950, China and the USSR signed a treaty of friendship. Both countries promised to assist and defend one another:

- The Soviet Union gave China a loan of $300 million.
- Soviet experts and advisors were sent to help modernise China.
- Both countries agreed to defend one another if they were attacked by Japan, or a country associated with Japan. This was an indirect threat to America, as it was a Japanese ally.

> **Comment and Analysis**
>
> The alliance between the USSR and China harmed East-West relations. The USA felt threatened — they began to believe that Stalin had always intended to ally himself with China, and that the USSR was co-ordinating an international communist movement.

4) The USA had hoped that China wouldn't become a Soviet ally when Mao took power. They wanted Mao's China to be like Tito's Yugoslavia (see p.10) — a communist state outside of the USSR's control.

The USA feared that Communism would Spread in Asia

1) Truman was worried that the 'fall' of China to communism would lead other Asian countries to become communist.

2) The USA's policy of containment (see p.10) had been focused on Europe. More limited efforts to contain communism had been carried out in Asia, such as giving aid to the Chinese Nationalists — but this effort in China had failed.

> The USA had success in Japan, though — by 1950, it had turned Japan into a thriving capitalist democracy. It was hoped that this would encourage other Asian countries to reject communism.

3) Some American politicians blamed Mao's success on Truman, accusing him of not being tough enough on communism. In response, Truman agreed to implement National Security Council Paper 68 (NSC-68):

- NSC-68 was an American report completed in April 1950. It warned that the Soviet Union aimed to dominate both Europe and Asia.
- It recommended that the USA should be more aggressive in its effort to defend non-communist countries against the Soviet threat.
- NSC-68 prompted the US to expand its military and nuclear weaponry.

> **Comment and Analysis**
>
> The USA also felt threatened by the Soviets' development of the atomic bomb in August 1949 (p.22). This made NSC-68 more appealing.

The USSR and China

Try these activities for a recap of the USSR's relationship with China and an in-depth look at some sources.

Knowledge and Understanding

1) Explain how China became a communist country. Give as much detail as possible.

2) What did the USSR and China agree in their treaty of friendship in 1950?

3) In your own words, explain what NSC-68 was. Give as much detail as you can.

Source Analysis

Source A

An American cartoon, published in 1951. The man standing on top of the globe represents the USSR.

Source B
The fundamental design* of those who control the Soviet Union and the international communist movement is to retain and solidify their absolute power, first in the Soviet Union and second in the areas now under their control...
The design... calls for the complete subversion** or forcible destruction of the machinery of government and structure of society in the countries of the non-Soviet world... Soviet efforts are now directed toward the domination of the Eurasian*** land mass.

*basic aim   **ruin   ***European and Asian

An extract from NSC-68, completed in April 1950.

1) Source A is critical of the USSR's foreign policy. Find two details from the cartoon that show this and explain your answers.

2) Explain how useful Source A would be for studying the USSR's actions in Asia.
You should write about the following features of the source in your answer:

The content of the source   The date of the source   Who produced the source

3) Explain how the content, date and authorship of Source B affect its usefulness for studying the USSR's actions in Asia.

EXAM TIP

I use a policy of containment when my sentences are too long...
You'll be asked to write about the usefulness of sources in question 2 in the exam. Think about the specific features of each source that make it useful for the investigation you've been given.

Korea and Vietnam

By the 1950s, the focus of the Cold War had shifted to Asia. The USA worried that communism could spread throughout Asia and undermine US power — this fear is reflected in America's actions in Korea and Vietnam.

The Korean War broke out in June 1950...

Korea was liberated from Japanese occupation in 1945. The country was temporarily split to help it recover — it was occupied by Soviet forces in the North, and US forces in the South. Both powers promoted their political ideologies in these regions, and efforts to reunify the country failed.

1) In 1948, two separate governments were established in Korea. Communist North Korea was led by Kim Il-sung and backed by the USSR, and anti-communist South Korea was led by Syngman Rhee and backed by the USA. Both leaders wanted to unite Korea and spread their beliefs across the whole country.

2) War broke out in June 1950 after Stalin agreed to support an invasion of South Korea by North Korea, and provide Kim Il-sung with weapons.

3) When South Korea turned to the UN Security Council for help, the USA proposed that the UN should support them. The USSR was not present to veto (reject) this, so the proposal was passed.

The USSR had stopped attending UN Security Council meetings to protest the UN's refusal to recognise communist China.

4) UN forces entered the conflict. The majority were South Korean and American, and their leader was US general Douglas MacArthur.

5) The Soviet Union supported North Korea against the UN forces, providing them with aircraft, tanks and artillery.

6) MacArthur suggested using atomic weapons, but America wasn't prepared to risk nuclear war. MacArthur was fired in 1951.

Comment and Analysis

The conflict in Korea was a proxy war between the USA and the USSR — the two powers supported opposite sides of the conflict, but didn't personally declare war on each other.

7) The war became a stalemate, with neither side making significant progress. Both sides agreed to a truce in 1953 — North Korea remained communist and South Korea stayed non-communist.

... and a Similar situation was unfolding in Vietnam

1) Vietnam was part of a French colony called Indochina. In the 1940s, the Viet Minh, a group of rebels who opposed French rule in Vietnam, gained influence. They were led by the communist, Ho Chi Minh.

2) The USSR and China recognised Ho Chi Minh as the legitimate leader of Vietnam in January 1950.

3) The USA became increasingly convinced that if Vietnam 'fell' to communism, other countries in Southeast Asia would follow and the region would become a Soviet stronghold.

This belief became known as the domino theory.

4) America sent aid to the French to help them resist the Viet Minh. However, the French were defeated in May 1954. It was then decided that Vietnam should be temporarily split to form communist North Vietnam, led by Ho Chi Minh, and South Vietnam.

5) The USA helped to install the anti-communist leader, Ngo Dinh Diem, in South Vietnam in 1955. Attempts to overthrow Diem were made by the Vietcong, a communist force in South Vietnam which was backed by the North. In response, the USA sent aid and thousands of military advisors to help Diem.

6) Diem was overthrown and assassinated by his own military in 1963. As political instability in South Vietnam continued, American involvement increased — in 1965, the first US combat troops were sent to Vietnam. By 1968, there were over 500,000 American troops in Vietnam.

Comment and Analysis

Vietnam contributed to Cold War tensions. The USA saw it as evidence that Soviet-backed communism was spreading, while the USSR criticised the USA for its aggressive actions.

7) The USSR and China supported North Vietnam and the Vietcong. As the USA increased its presence in the South, the USSR gave more aid to the North, providing weapons such as missiles and radar systems.

8) Involvement in Vietnam became disastrous for America, and US troops finally withdrew without victory in 1973. Vietnam became a united, communist country in 1975, but Southeast Asia did not 'fall' to communism as the US government had feared.

Korea and Vietnam

There were important differences between the conflicts in Korea and Vietnam, but also some key similarities. Have a go at the activities on this page to help you learn the key facts about why there was tension in Asia.

Knowledge and Understanding

1) Describe the situation in Korea between 1945 and the outbreak of war in June 1950.

2) Explain how the UN became involved in the Korean War.

3) What was the outcome of the Korean War?

4) Write a definition for each of the following key terms:

   a) proxy war   b) Indochina   c) the Viet Minh   d) the domino theory   e) the Vietcong

5) Copy and complete the timeline below about the Vietnam War by describing the developments that happened in each year.

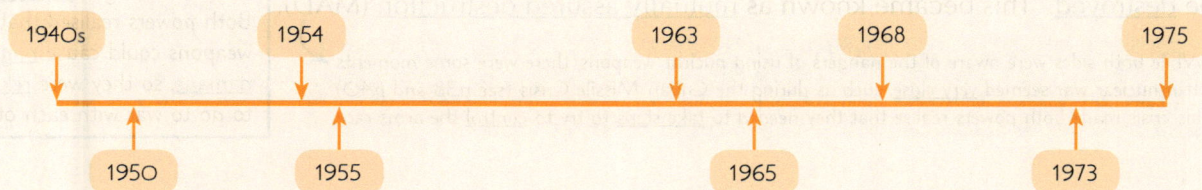

1940s	1954	1963	1968	1975

1950	1955	1965	1973

Thinking Historically

1) Copy and complete the table below, listing the actions taken by the USA and the USSR that increased tension between the two superpowers over Asia. Use information from pages 18 and 20.

Actions taken by the USA	Actions taken by the USSR

2) Using your completed table to help you, explain whether you think the main reason for Cold War tensions in Asia was the actions taken by the USA or the actions taken by the USSR.

The Vietnam War was a disaster for the USA...

To get top marks in question 4 in the exam, try to make links between different factors. Understanding how they are related will help you to judge which one was most important.

Military Rivalries

During the Cold War, the USA and the USSR tried to gain an advantage by developing ever more powerful weapons. The aim was to 'look strong' to deter the other from attacking.

The USA and the USSR began an Arms Race

1) The USA was the only nuclear power in the world when it used atomic bombs in Japan in 1945 (see p.8). Possession of this powerful weapon gave America an advantage over the Soviet Union.

2) As tensions rose between America and the USSR after the Second World War, the Soviets intensified their efforts to develop nuclear weapons — the USSR wanted security and to compete with the USA. However, America was determined to maintain its nuclear superiority.

3) This meant that during the Cold War, the USA and the USSR worked to develop the most powerful weapons they could — there was an arms race.

> The USA and the USSR both worried that the other might use its nuclear weapons — this caused fear and suspicion on both sides.

4) Neither side really wanted to use these weapons, but both felt the other couldn't be allowed to gain an advantage. The fear was that if either gained a significant military advantage, that country might be tempted to trigger a war.

5) This led to an intense rivalry, where both powers constantly tried to develop more powerful and more dangerous weapons.

6) By the late 1950s, the USA and the USSR had the power to destroy each other several times over. This began to act as a deterrent — if one nation used nuclear weapons and the other retaliated, both nations would be destroyed. This became known as mutually assured destruction (MAD).

Comment and Analysis

Some historians think that the arms race prevented the Cold War from becoming a physical conflict. Both powers realised that their weapons could cause huge damage, so they were reluctant to go to war with each other.

> While both sides were aware of the dangers of using nuclear weapons, there were some moments when nuclear war seemed very close, such as during the Cuban Missile Crisis (see p.38 and p.40). This crisis made both powers realise that they needed to take steps to try to control the arms race.

Both countries developed Nuclear Stockpiles

1) The USA and the USSR both developed more powerful weapons as they tried to keep up with each other:

- The USA developed its atom bomb during the Second World War and used it against Japan in 1945.
- The USSR wasn't far behind, and in 1949 succeeded in exploding its own atom bomb.
- The USA detonated the first hydrogen bomb (another type of nuclear bomb) in 1952. This bomb was around 500 times more powerful than those which the USA had dropped on Japan in 1945.

> The USA was surprised by how quickly the USSR developed its atom bomb.

- The USSR began testing hydrogen bombs in 1953. By 1955 it had developed its own powerful design.
- In August 1957, the Soviets successfully tested the first Intercontinental Ballistic Missile (ICBM), which could strike the USA after being launched from the USSR. ICBMs were virtually unstoppable.
- The USA had started researching ICBMs in 1946, but its first successful ICBM test only took place in 1959. America then quickly increased its stock of these missiles until it had a significant advantage over the USSR.

> The USSR began catching up again, as American resources were diverted into the war with Vietnam (see p.20).

- In 1960, the USA deployed submarines which carried Polaris missiles. These missiles could be fired from anywhere under the sea, and the submarines were hard to detect.

2) The arms race was also fuelled by the fear and suspicion created by other events:

- The formation of NATO (see p.24) in 1949 made the USSR feel militarily vulnerable.
- In February 1950, communist China and the USSR signed a treaty of friendship (see p.13), which strengthened Western fears that the USSR was planning communist domination.

Military Rivalries

These activities will help you learn the reasons for the arms race, how it developed and its consequences.

Knowledge and Understanding

1) Explain what is meant by the term 'arms race'.

2) Explain why the USSR wanted to develop nuclear weapons after 1945.

The graph below shows the changing nuclear capability of the USA and the USSR over time.
The USA is represented by the blue line and the USSR is represented by the red line.

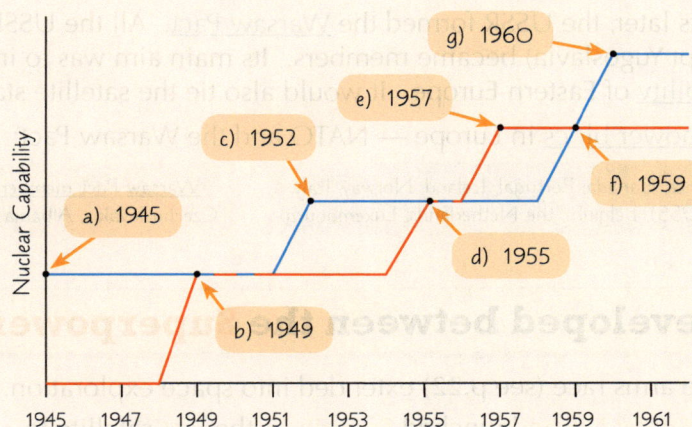

a) 1945   b) 1949   c) 1952   d) 1955   e) 1957   f) 1959   g) 1960

Nuclear Capability

1945 1947 1949 1951 1953 1955 1957 1959 1961

3) Copy and complete the graph, adding details about the military developments that happened in each of the years labelled. Try to include as much information as possible.

4) Copy and complete the mind map below, explaining how each factor fuelled the arms race between the USA and the USSR.

a) The formation of NATO   ←   Causes of the arms race   →   b) The treaty of friendship between China and the USSR

Thinking Historically

1) Explain how the arms race affected relations between the USA and the USSR.
Include the following key words or phrases in your answer:

fear and suspicion   rivalry   mutually assured destruction

The rivalry between the USA and the USSR kept on going...

*Remember that there were similarities as well as differences between the USA and the USSR.
Their achievements differed, but they shared similar aims and were equally afraid of each other.*

Military Rivalries

The USA and the USSR also competed through forming military alliances and carrying out space exploration.

The Two Powers established Military Alliances

1) Stalin's blockade during the Berlin crisis (see p.12) showed how unprepared the West would be if there was a conflict with the USSR.

2) As a result, the Western Powers formed a military alliance. In April 1949, NATO (the North Atlantic Treaty Organisation) was created. All members of NATO agreed to respond together if any member of the alliance was attacked.

Comment and Analysis

Western European nations wanted support, so asked the USA to form NATO. This was the first time America agreed to defend Europe during peacetime.

Warsaw Pact members formed the so-called 'Eastern Bloc'.

3) The Soviets saw NATO as a real threat. When West Germany joined NATO in 1955 and began to rearm, the USSR decided to act — it was worried that NATO was becoming stronger and that West Germany was now a danger to the security of the USSR.

4) Weeks later, the USSR formed the Warsaw Pact. All the USSR's satellite states (except Yugoslavia) became members. Its main aim was to improve the defensive capability of Eastern Europe. It would also tie the satellite states closer to the USSR.

5) There were now two power blocs in Europe — NATO and the Warsaw Pact:

NATO members: USA, UK, France, Canada, Portugal, Iceland, Norway, Italy, Denmark, West Germany (from 1955), Belgium, the Netherlands, Luxembourg.

Warsaw Pact members: USSR, Poland, Hungary, Bulgaria, Czechoslovakia, Albania (until 1968), Romania, East Germany.

A Space Race developed between the Superpowers

1) The rivalry fuelling the arms race (see p.22) extended into space exploration.

2) In October 1957, the Soviet Union launched Sputnik — the first satellite to be sent into space. The USSR saw this as a victory over America. The USA rushed to launch its own satellite — the 'space race' had begun.

3) The US satellite, Explorer 1, was launched in January 1958. In July 1958, President Eisenhower founded the National Aeronautics and Space Administration (NASA), which focused on space research and exploration.

Comment and Analysis

The USSR took an early lead in the space race. This shocked Americans, who had assumed that their scientific research was more advanced.

4) The USSR made more progress in April 1961, when Yuri Gagarin became the first person to travel into space. A month later, the USA sent an American, Alan Shepard, into space for the first time.

© Chronicle / Alamy Stock Photo

5) In May 1961, President Kennedy claimed that the USA would put a man on the Moon by the end of the decade.

6) In the early 1960s, the US government increased NASA's annual budget from $500 million to $5.2 billion. Plans for Project Apollo, a US mission to the Moon, began to take shape during this time. Apollo missions took place throughout the decade, and finally in 1969, Apollo 11 was successful — Neil Armstrong and Buzz Aldrin became the first men to walk on the Moon.

After the Moon landing, the USA claimed to have won the space race.

The space race caused Tensions to Escalate Further

1) The space race fuelled yet more competition between the USA and the USSR. Success in the space race became linked to power and status — the superpower that seemed more technologically advanced could be seen by the rest of the world as being the superior power.

The USSR's early achievements in the space race worried the USA — Americans thought Soviet success might make people think communism was superior to capitalism.

2) The space race also intensified the arms race. The rockets used to launch satellites were also capable of carrying ICBMs (see p.22) — the USSR's use of a rocket to launch Sputnik made it clear to Americans that the Soviets were also capable of reaching the USA with nuclear weapons. Fears of a nuclear attack increased, and the USA sped up its weapons programmes.

Military Rivalries

This page will give you the chance to compare two sources and learn the key facts about the space race.

Source Analysis

Source A is a cartoon from a Soviet magazine, published in 1949. The man at the top represents the USA, and the other men represent Western European countries. The men are signing a treaty to become members of NATO.

1) The cartoon is critical of NATO. Explain how each of the details below shows this.

   a) The USA is sitting on top of Western European countries as they all sign the treaty.

   b) The USA is holding an atom bomb.

Source A

Source B

NATO has become one of the most powerful facts of international life. It is the foundation of the structure of security the free nations are building around the world... The Soviet Union has forced its satellites into an involuntary alliance held together by force and fear. This is the old system of domination and dictatorship. NATO is the new concept. Twelve European countries with Canada and the United States have voluntarily come together as free and equal partners, eager to work out common solutions to common problems.

Source B is from a speech given by US politician Averell Harriman in April 1952.

2) Why do you think Source A and Source B have different opinions about NATO?

3) Why do you think the sources might be useful as a pair for investigating opinions about NATO? Explain your answer.

Knowledge and Understanding

1) Make a timeline for the period 1957-1969, showing all the main developments in the space race between the USA and the USSR. Try to include as much detail as possible.

There's an example of a timeline on page 21.

2) Explain why success in the space race was important to the USA and the USSR.

3) How did the space race affect the arms race? Explain your answer.

 **EXAM TIP**

The USSR wasn't exactly over the moon about Apollo 11...

When you're analysing the sources in question 2 in the exam, you need to write about how useful each source is on its own, but you should also consider how useful they are as a pair.

The 'Thaw'

When Khrushchev became leader of the USSR in 1953, there were hopes of a 'thaw' in the Cold War. Many thought that East-West relations would improve and that Soviet satellite states would have more freedom.

Khrushchev aimed to Reform the Soviet Union

1) In March 1953, Stalin died. His regime had been repressive — his secret police arrested anyone who was seen as a threat to communism. Those who were arrested were often killed, or sent to labour camps.

2) In September 1953, another member of the Communist Party, Nikita Khrushchev, became the leader of the USSR. He wanted his party to focus on improving life in the USSR, and ensuring that the population benefitted more than they would under capitalism.

3) In 1956, Khrushchev made a speech criticising Stalin's policies — this shocked communists around the world. Khrushchev brought in measures to 'de-Stalinise' the USSR:

- Many prisoners jailed under Stalin were released and the death penalty was abolished.
- Stalin's secret police had their powers limited.
- Statues of Stalin were taken down.

> De-Stalinisation was popular with the Western Powers — they disliked Stalin's style of rule and hoped that the USSR's control over its own people and its satellites might now weaken.

Khrushchev raised hopes of 'Peaceful Co-existence'

1) In January 1953, Dwight D. Eisenhower had succeeded Truman as US President. With new leaders in both the Soviet Union and the USA, there was an opportunity for a fresh start between the superpowers.

2) Khrushchev said that he believed in 'peaceful co-existence' — that capitalist and communist countries could exist together without conflict. This contrasted with Stalin's belief that war between them was inevitable.

3) Khrushchev's words created hope that relations between the USA and the USSR would improve and that there would be a 'thaw' in Cold War tensions. Some developments took place to encourage better relations:

Eisenhower and Khrushchev shaking hands.

- The USA and the USSR met in Geneva in 1955 and agreed to communicate more openly.
- In 1955, the USSR officially recognised the Federal Republic of Germany (West Germany) as a state.

4) However, Khrushchev remained very competitive with the USA. He wanted communism to spread, but believed that the best way to achieve this was to demonstrate communism's superiority — not defeat the West in a war.

> **Comment and Analysis**
>
> Khrushchev continued to develop weapons, which meant that the West still felt threatened.

Unrest began to Stir in the Eastern Bloc

> Communism created a lot of economic hardship — poor living conditions increased anti-Soviet sentiment.

1) Some satellite states hoped that their countries would also become 'de-Stalinised'. Khrushchev abolished Cominform (see p.10), meaning that states in Eastern Europe would have more political and economic freedom from the USSR.

> **Comment and Analysis**
>
> Khrushchev wanted the Eastern Bloc to remain communist — he just didn't agree with Stalin's approach to communism. He thought that giving satellite states more economic independence would stabilise their communist regimes, but his plan backfired.

2) De-Stalinisation allowed tensions in the satellite states to rise to the surface. Not all states had chosen communism, and saw the changes as a chance to loosen ties with the USSR.

3) In 1956, there was an uprising in Poland. The USSR threatened to intervene, but eventually allowed the new government to follow their own version of communism. This encouraged other states, such as Hungary (see p.28), to consider revolt.

The 'Thaw'

After Stalin's death, there were important changes to the balance of the Cold War. Have a go at these activities to test your knowledge of why there was a 'thaw' in relations and why tension still remained.

Knowledge and Understanding

1) Copy and complete the mind map below about the actions Khrushchev took to 'de-Stalinise' the USSR.

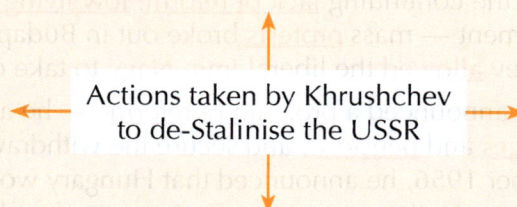

Actions taken by Khrushchev to de-Stalinise the USSR

2) Explain how Khrushchev's opinion differed to Stalin's on the following issues:
   a) The likelihood of war between capitalist and communist countries
   b) How to control the Eastern Bloc

3) Give one reason why the West still felt threatened by the USSR, even after Khrushchev came to power.

4) How did economic hardship contribute to tension in Eastern Europe?

Thinking Historically

1) Copy and complete the mind map below, explaining how each factor contributed to a 'thaw' in Cold War tensions. Give as much detail in your answers as possible.

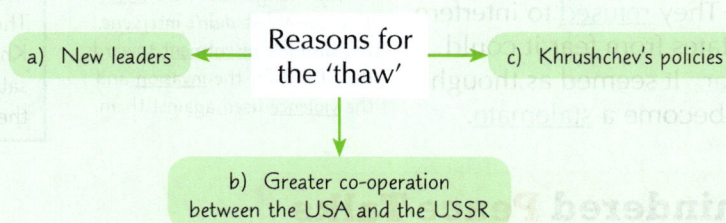

Reasons for the 'thaw'

a) New leaders

c) Khrushchev's policies

b) Greater co-operation between the USA and the USSR

2) Copy and complete the flow chart below, explaining the consequences of each stage in the growth of unrest in Eastern Europe.

Khrushchev begins de-Stalinisation. → a) Consequences: → There is an uprising in Poland in 1956. → b) Consequences:

EXAM TIP

Khrushchev's favourite Norse god was definitely Thor...

When starting a new paragraph in longer answers, begin by referring back to the question. This will help you make sure you're answering the question and all your points are relevant.

Hungary and the U2 Crisis

The Soviet policy of 'peaceful co-existence' was challenged by the Hungarian Uprising and the U2 Crisis.

The USSR used the Hungarian Uprising to send a Message

1) After World War Two, the USSR helped put Mátyás Rákosi, a brutal Stalinist, in charge of Hungary. His authoritarian regime became increasingly unpopular, so he was removed from power and replaced with Erno Gero in July 1956.

> De-Stalinisation and the Polish uprising (see p.26) encouraged Hungarians to ask for reform.

2) People became frustrated by the continuing lack of reform, low living standards and Soviet control under Gero's government — mass protests broke out in Budapest in October 1956. To end these riots, Khrushchev allowed the liberal Imre Nagy to take over from Gero.

> The USSR wasn't aware of Nagy's wish to leave the Warsaw Pact and become neutral until he made this announcement.

3) Nagy soon announced a program of reforms — he aimed to dissolve the secret police, review wages and pensions, and secure the withdrawal of Soviet troops from Hungary. In November 1956, he announced that Hungary would withdraw from the Warsaw Pact and hold free elections — ending Soviet control and turning Hungary into a neutral state.

4) If Hungary was allowed to turn away from communism, other satellite states might do the same. The USSR felt it had to respond with force and make an example of Nagy.

5) Khrushchev, who had only held power for two years, also wanted to use the crisis to assert his authority.

6) Soviet tanks invaded Hungary in November 1956. Thousands of Hungarians were killed or wounded. Nagy was arrested and hanged. János Kádár replaced Nagy and ensured loyalty towards the USSR.

The West Condemned the Soviets, but No Action was taken against them

1) Western countries criticised the Soviet Union for the invasion of Hungary — they were shocked by the USSR's use of violence against the Hungarian people.

2) The invasion undermined 'peaceful co-existence' in the eyes of the West. Although Khrushchev had said that he felt the East and the West could exist together peacefully, the invasion of Hungary showed that the USSR could still be aggressive and wasn't afraid to use violence to protect communism.

3) The USA and its allies took the issue of the USSR's involvement in Hungary to the United Nations. The members of the UN held a vote on whether the USSR should withdraw from Hungary, but the USSR vetoed (rejected) the vote and no action was taken.

4) Western nations took no further action against the USSR. They refused to interfere with the satellite states from fear it could cause a nuclear war. It seemed as though the Cold War had become a stalemate.

> Many Hungarians were angry that the West didn't intervene. They also felt resentment towards the USSR for the invasion and the violence used against them.

Comment and Analysis

It was clear that the Cold War wasn't over — Khrushchev was determined to keep a tight grip on the USSR's sphere of influence. The invasion had brutally reasserted Khrushchev's authority over the satellite states and strengthened the position of the USSR.

The U2 Crisis hindered Peace Talks

1) President Eisenhower and Khrushchev had agreed to discuss issues such as controls on nuclear weapon testing and the situation in Berlin (see p.34) at the Paris Peace Summit in 1960. On 1st May, days before the summit was due to take place, the USSR shot down a U2 American spy plane over Soviet territory. The plane had been collecting information on the USSR's military facilities.

2) At first, Eisenhower denied that it was a spy plane. However, the USSR produced the pilot, Gary Powers, and the plane's wreckage as evidence that Eisenhower had lied. The US government then admitted that Powers had been flying a US spy plane.

> Gary Powers was sentenced to ten years in a Soviet prison for spying. However, Powers was returned to the USA in exchange for a Soviet spy after less than two years.

3) Khrushchev demanded an apology from Eisenhower, but he refused — Eisenhower argued that the use of spy planes was necessary to help the USA protect itself against attacks.

4) Khrushchev walked out of the Paris Peace Summit before talks could begin. He also cancelled a trip Eisenhower was due to take to the USSR which had been planned for the following month.

The Development of the Cold War

Hungary and the U2 Crisis

Use this page to check you understand how the invasion of Hungary and the U2 crisis worsened relations.

Thinking Historically

1) Copy and complete the flowchart below, explaining the consequences of each stage leading up to the Soviet invasion of Hungary in November 1956.

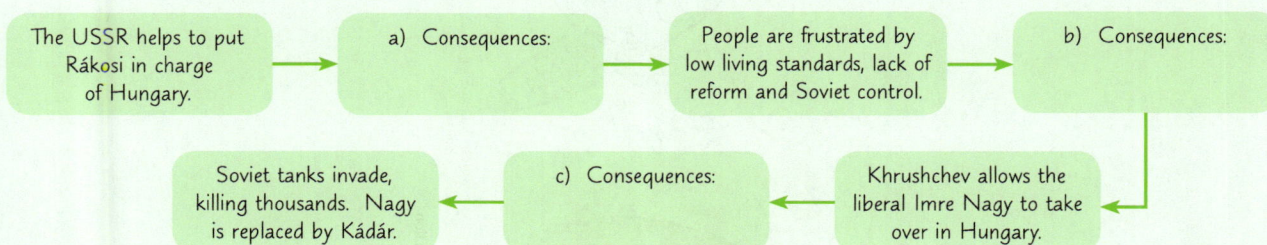

The USSR helps to put Rákosi in charge of Hungary.	→	a) Consequences:	→	People are frustrated by low living standards, lack of reform and Soviet control.	→	b) Consequences:

Soviet tanks invade, killing thousands. Nagy is replaced by Kádár.	←	c) Consequences:	←	Khrushchev allows the liberal Imre Nagy to take over in Hungary.	←	

2) Explain the consequences of the Soviet invasion of Hungary for the following:

a) Relations between the East and the West   b) Soviet authority in Eastern Europe

3) Explain how the U2 crisis worsened relations between the USA and the USSR. Include as much detail as possible in your answer.

Source Analysis

The source below is an extract from a speech made by President Eisenhower at a news conference about the U2 crisis on 11th May 1960.

> ... we must have knowledge of military forces and preparations around the world, especially those capable of massive surprise attack. Secrecy in the Soviet Union makes this essential. In most of the world no large-scale attack could be prepared in secret. But in the Soviet Union there is a fetish* of secrecy and concealment. This is a major cause of international tension and uneasiness today. Our deterrent must never be placed in jeopardy**. The safety of the whole free world demands this.

*devotion to   **danger

1) Imagine you are using this source for an investigation into the U2 crisis. Explain how the features listed below affect its usefulness for your investigation.

a) Author   b) Purpose   c) Date   d) Content

EXAM TIP

The USSR kept a tight hold of its satellite states...

When you're writing about causes or consequences, you can use linking words and phrases such as 'therefore', 'as a result' and 'because of this' to show the connections between events.

Worked Exam-Style Questions

Have a look at these sample answers — they'll help you to analyse sources and write narrative accounts.

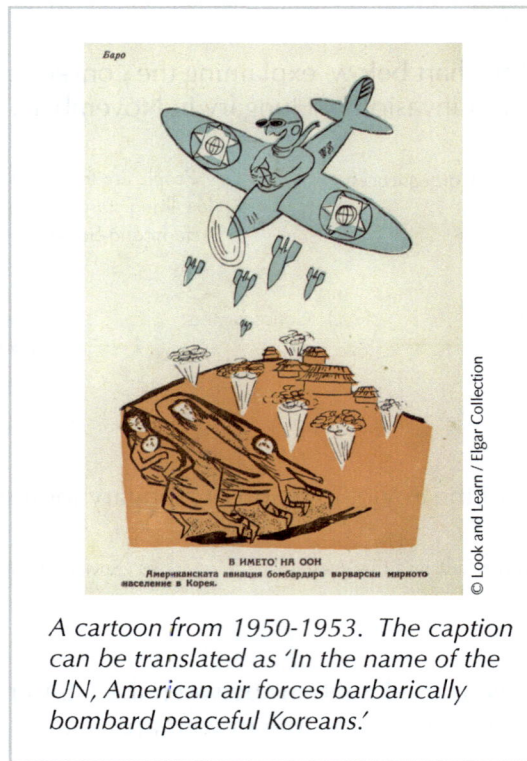

A cartoon from 1950-1953. The caption can be translated as 'In the name of the UN, American air forces barbarically bombard peaceful Koreans.'

© Look and Learn / Elgar Collection

How can you tell that the source above is critical of America's involvement in Korea? Use the source and your own knowledge to explain your answer.   [4 marks]

> We can tell that the source is critical of America's involvement in Korea because it makes the US armed forces who were helping non-communist South Korea fight communist North Korea during the Korean War seem inhumane and cruel. The source does this by accusing the US air forces of 'barbarically' attacking 'peaceful Koreans', and showing an American pilot laughing as he drops bombs on a Korean village and a fleeing family.
>   We can tell that the source is also critical of the way in which the USA became involved in Korea. The caption states that American troops were acting 'In the name of the UN', suggesting that the USA acted in Korea under the cover of helping the United Nations. America had proposed that the UN should help defend South Korea against the communist North because it was concerned about the spread of communism in Asia. UN forces entered the conflict, but they were led by a US general, and many of the soldiers were American. Therefore, we can tell that the source is critical of America's involvement in Korea because it is suggesting that the USA entered the Korean War and cruelly attacked civilians to further its own Cold War interests.

Identify different features of the source and explain why they have been included.

Make sure you use your own knowledge to help explain what the source shows.

This links analysis of the source back to the question.

Worked Exam-Style Questions

Give an account of how the creation of NATO in 1949 increased tensions between the USA and the USSR.   [8 marks]

This addresses the question in the first sentence.

The creation of NATO in 1949 increased tensions between the USA and the USSR by heightening the fear and suspicion between the superpowers and strengthening the divide between the East and the West.

The formation of NATO increased tensions between America and the USSR by making the Western powers seem more threatening to the USSR. NATO meant that there was now an agreement in place that would help the West act together if the USSR attacked a member state. When West Germany joined NATO in 1955 and began to rearm, the Soviets felt even more intimidated. They were concerned that NATO was becoming more powerful and that West Germany now posed a serious threat to the USSR. As a result, the USSR created its own military alliance with its satellite states (except Yugoslavia) through the Warsaw Pact. This caused tensions between the powers to grow, as both countries increasingly interpreted each other's actions as threatening.

This makes it clear that one development led to another.

This explains how this consequence of the creation of NATO increased tensions between America and the USSR.

The creation of NATO also increased tensions between the USA and the USSR by leading to the formation of two opposing sides in the Cold War. The Western powers were united through NATO, and six years later, the Warsaw Pact formally united the USSR and its satellite states, creating the Eastern Bloc. This meant that there were now two rival groups of powers that were bound by military alliances to act against one another if either side attacked the other. This increased tensions because it created a more formal military division between the East and West, and increased the risk of active conflict between the two sides.

This introduces another reason why NATO increased tensions between the superpowers.

Use relevant knowledge to back up your points.

The creation of NATO contributed to the development of the arms race, which also increased tensions between the USA and the USSR. Because the military alliance of the Western powers through NATO made the USSR feel more vulnerable, it invested more in trying to beat the USA in the arms race, which led to the launch of the first ICBM in 1957. This rivalry and the development of ever more powerful weapons led both powers to feel threatened, and they became increasingly suspicious of each other.

This introduces another key factor that's relevant to the issue in the question.

This explains why this consequence was significant.

Overall, the creation of NATO increased tensions between the USA and the Soviet Union by heightening the fear and suspicion that divided the superpowers and by formalising the division between the East and the West into two opposing sides. It also resulted in the acceleration of the arms race, which caused further tensions between the USA and the USSR.

This gives a clear answer to the question.

This sums up why the creation of NATO increased tensions between the USA and the USSR.

Exam-Style Questions

Now that you know all about how the Cold War developed, get stuck into these exam-style questions.

Source A

A poster published by the USSR in 1961. The man in the spacesuit is Yuri Gagarin. The text can be translated as 'Long live Soviet science! Long live Soviet man — the first cosmonaut!'

© Stocktrek / Mary Evans

Source B

Comments made by President Eisenhower in April 1954 at a news conference. He is discussing his concerns that if Indochina (an area of Asia that included Vietnam) became communist, other countries in Asia would follow — this became known as the 'domino theory'.

Finally, you have broader considerations that might follow what you would call the 'falling domino' principle. You have a row of dominoes set up, you knock over the first one, and what will happen to the last one is the certainty that it will go over very quickly. So you could have a beginning of a disintegration that would have the most profound* influences... Asia, after all, has already lost some 450 million of its peoples to the Communist dictatorship, and we simply can't afford greater losses. But when we come to the possible sequence of events, the loss of Indochina, of Burma, of Thailand... and Indonesia... now you are talking really about millions and millions and millions of people. Finally, the geographical position achieved thereby does many things. It turns the so-called island defensive chain** of Japan, Formosa***, of the Philippines and to the southward; it moves in to threaten Australia and New Zealand... So, the possible consequences of the loss are just incalculable to the free world.

*serious

**Islands around China which the USA believed could help defend against the spread of communism.

***An old name for Taiwan.

The Development of the Cold War

Exam-Style Questions

Source C

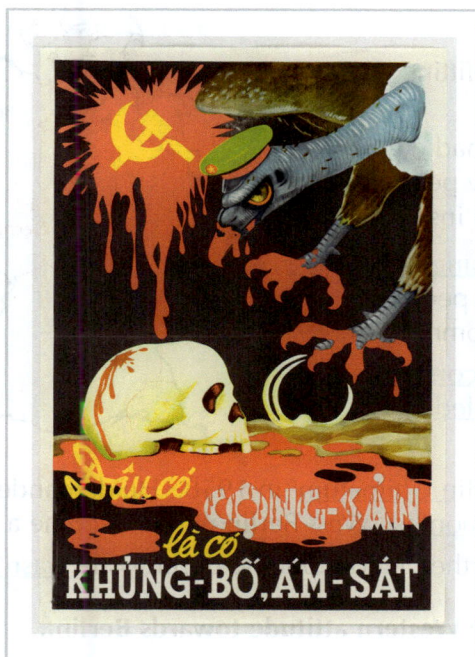

An American poster which was produced shortly after the decision to divide Vietnam into North Vietnam and South Vietnam in July 1954.

The poster was produced by the United States Information Agency, an organisation established by President Eisenhower in 1953.

The poster was published in South Vietnam. The text can be translated as 'Anywhere there is communism, there is terrorism and assassination!'

Exam-Style Questions

1) How can you tell that Source A supports the USSR's achievements in the space race? Use Source A and your own knowledge to explain your answer.   [4 marks]

2) Look at Source B and Source C. How useful would these sources be to a historian studying the spread of communism in Asia? Use both sources and your own knowledge to explain your answer.   [12 marks]

3) Give an account of how the arms race increased tensions between the Soviet Union and the USA.   [8 marks]

4) 'The Hungarian Uprising was the main reason why East-West relations worsened between 1950 and 1960.'

   Explain how far you agree with this statement.   [16 marks]

For the 16-mark question in the exam, 4 extra marks will be available for spelling, punctuation, grammar and using specialist terminology.

The Berlin Question

The two superpowers tried to resolve the situation in Berlin, but by the 1960s the issue had worsened.

Berlin remained a Source of Tension

1) After the Berlin crisis in 1948 (see p.12), West Berlin was a unified zone and continued to develop economically, benefitting from a new currency and American (Marshall Plan) aid.

2) The situation in East Berlin was very different — the USSR had drained it of resources and its economy was slow to develop. Many people wanted to leave and go to the more prosperous West Berlin instead.

> By 1961, at least 3 million East Germans had emigrated from East Berlin to West Berlin.

3) The situation was hugely embarrassing for Khrushchev, as it suggested that people preferred life under capitalism to communism.

4) It also threatened East Germany's economy, as many of those who left were skilled workers in search of a better life.

5) The refugee crisis in Berlin led Khrushchev to issue his 'Berlin Ultimatum' in 1958. He demanded that US, British and French troops leave West Berlin within six months. West Berlin would become a free city.

6) Eisenhower refused the ultimatum. Khrushchev took no further action, but the Berlin issue wasn't solved.

The Soviet attitude towards Berlin...

- The USSR felt threatened by the economic success in West Berlin.
- East Berlin had become dependent on trade links with West Berlin.
- The USSR worried the West was trying to use its strong economy to interfere in Eastern Europe.

The Western attitude towards Berlin...

- After the Berlin Airlift, West Berlin became a symbol of democracy — it had to be supported or the West would lose credibility.
- People fleeing from East Berlin suited the West — it was good propaganda because it made communism look weak.

Khrushchev and Eisenhower held a Summit in 1959

1) In 1959, Khrushchev became the first communist leader to visit the USA. The meeting symbolised a new spirit of co-operation and communication between the two powers.

2) At the meeting they discussed Berlin. Eisenhower still didn't agree to withdraw from West Berlin, but did agree to discuss the matter more deeply.

3) The leaders decided to meet in Paris the following year. Although no firm decisions had been made, the arrangement of another summit promised to continue the optimistic dialogue they had started.

Talks about Berlin Broke Down

1) President Eisenhower and Khrushchev had agreed to discuss the situation in Berlin at the Paris Peace Summit in May 1960. However, Khrushchev walked out of the summit when the USA refused to apologise for the U2 incident (see p.28).

2) Both countries met again at Vienna in June 1961 — by this time, John F. Kennedy had replaced Eisenhower as US President.

3) Kennedy had vowed to take a tougher approach towards communism. After Khrushchev threatened to deny the Allies access to Berlin and warned of the possibility of war, Kennedy promised to defend the rights of the USA in West Berlin. Both leaders refused to compromise, and no resolution was reached.

Comment and Analysis

After the Vienna Summit, the USSR believed that problems in Berlin wouldn't be resolved by negotiation. This sparked the creation of the Berlin Wall (p.36).

The Berlin Question

Although there was hope of the superpowers reaching an agreement about Berlin, neither side could find a solution. Have a go at these activities to make sure you understand the significance of the situation in Berlin.

Knowledge and Understanding

1) Using the information on the previous page, write a definition for each of the following terms:

   a) Refugee crisis   b) Berlin Ultimatum

2) Explain why conditions in East Berlin were worse than conditions in West Berlin in the 1950s. Use the following key words or phrases in your answer:

   unified zone   Marshall Plan   resources   slow economic development   skilled workers

3) Copy and complete the mind map below to show how the USSR and the West felt about Berlin before 1959. Try to include as much detail as possible.

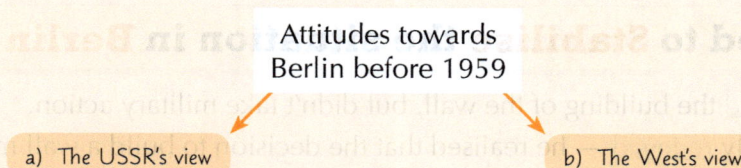

   Attitudes towards Berlin before 1959

   a) The USSR's view

   b) The West's view

4) Explain why the 1959 summit seemed like a positive step for East-West relations.

Thinking Historically

1) Copy and complete the flowchart below about the events after the refugee crisis in Berlin. Add as much information as you can under headings a) to d).

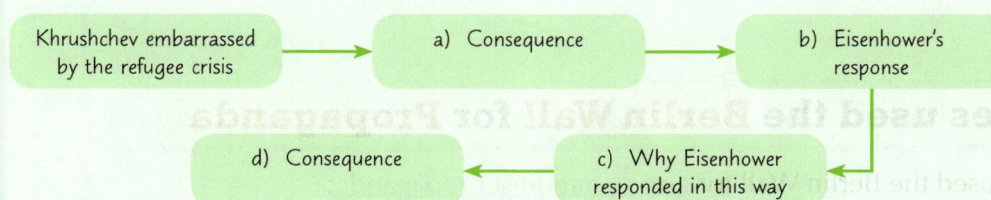

   Khrushchev embarrassed by the refugee crisis → a) Consequence → b) Eisenhower's response

   d) Consequence ← c) Why Eisenhower responded in this way

2) Give two reasons why talks about Berlin broke down after the 1959 summit and explain each one.

EXAM TIP

Both superpowers refused to compromise on Berlin...

Berlin was a key issue for both the West and the USSR. Neither side wanted to lose influence in the city, so both sides did everything they could to protect their rights in their zone of Berlin.

The Berlin Wall

In 1961, around 2000 Germans crossed over from East to West Berlin every day. When it became clear that the situation wasn't going to be solved diplomatically, Khrushchev constructed the Berlin Wall.

The Berlin Wall was Put Up in 1961

1) Khrushchev felt he had to act to stem the flow of refugees out of East Berlin. On 13th August 1961, a 27-mile barrier was built across the city of Berlin overnight, separating East from West.

2) It was fortified with barbed wire and machine gun posts, and was later strengthened and made into a more permanent barrier. Military checkpoints policed any movements into or out of East Berlin.

3) Before the wall, East Berliners had entered West Berlin freely. After the wall, they could no longer go to work in West Berlin and were instantly separated from friends and relatives.

4) Citizens from East and West Berlin were rarely allowed through the military checkpoints. Anyone who tried to escape East Berlin was shot.

A photo of the newly-built Berlin Wall.

© Mary Evans Picture Library/Imagno

The Wall helped to Stabilise the situation in Berlin

1) The USA condemned the building of the wall, but didn't take military action.

2) Kennedy was actually relieved — he realised that the decision to build a wall meant the USSR wasn't going to try to take West Berlin by force. He claimed that 'a wall is a hell of a lot better than a war'.

3) The wall succeeded in stopping mass emigration from East Berlin. It also gave East Germany the opportunity to rebuild its economy, and strengthen itself as a communist state.

4) However, there were still some tense moments between the superpowers — there was a military confrontation between the USA and the USSR in October 1961 at Checkpoint Charlie.

After the building of the wall, American troops and diplomats had been allowed to cross into East Berlin until East German border guards began to restrict their entry. The Americans responded by moving tanks up to Checkpoint Charlie, where they were met by Soviet tanks in a tense stand-off that lasted for around 16 hours. It seemed as though war might be a possibility, but neither side really wanted to risk conflict — Kennedy contacted Khrushchev and the two sides agreed to withdraw their tanks.

Comment and Analysis

Although the Berlin Wall helped to avoid open conflict, it became a symbol of the divide between East and West in the Cold War as a whole.

Both sides used the Berlin Wall for Propaganda

1) The USA used the Berlin Wall for anti-communist propaganda:

- The USA argued that the wall showed the failure of communism and saw it as a symbol of oppression — the only way the USSR could stop people leaving communist East Germany was to build a wall.

- Kennedy visited West Berlin in 1963 and gave a famous speech stating his solidarity with West Berlin and its people. He declared 'Ich bin ein Berliner' (I am a Berliner). He claimed that West Berlin represented freedom in the struggle against communism.

2) The East German government used propaganda to justify the building of the wall. They often called the Berlin Wall the 'Anti-fascist Protective Rampart', claiming that the wall was vital to national security because it kept out western spies.

The Berlin Wall

The activities on this page will help you understand the consequences of the construction of the Berlin Wall.

Knowledge and Understanding

1) Why did Khrushchev build the Berlin Wall? Use information from pages 34 and 36 to help you.

2) What happened at Checkpoint Charlie in October 1961?
Use the following key words and phrases in your answer:

| American troops and diplomats | border guards | tanks | 16 hours | withdraw |

Source Analysis

The source below is an extract from Kennedy's 'Ich bin ein Berliner' speech in West Berlin in 1963.

> There are many people in the world who really don't understand, or say they don't, what is the great issue between the free world and the Communist world. Let them come to Berlin. There are some who say that communism is the wave of the future. Let them come to Berlin... While the wall is the most obvious and vivid demonstration of the failures of the Communist system, for all the world to see, we take no satisfaction in it, for it is... an offense not only against history but an offense against humanity, separating families, dividing husbands and wives and brothers and sisters, and dividing a people who wish to be joined together.

1) Imagine you are using this source for an investigation into the USA's response to the construction of the Berlin Wall. Explain how each feature of the source listed below affects its usefulness for your investigation.

a) Author   b) Date   c) Purpose   d) Content

Thinking Historically

1) Copy and complete the mind map below about the consequences of the Berlin Wall being built.

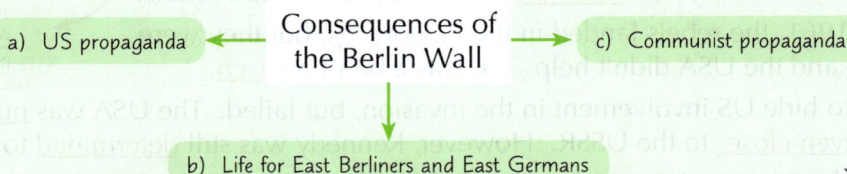

a) US propaganda ← Consequences of the Berlin Wall → c) Communist propaganda

b) Life for East Berliners and East Germans

Think about both the positive and negative effects on East-West relations.

2) Explain how the construction of the Berlin Wall affected East-West relations.

EXAM TIP

The wall cemented the divide between East and West...

The construction of the Berlin Wall was a really significant point in the Cold War. It's important that you know about the events that led up to it, and what it meant for the USA and the USSR.

The Cuban Missile Crisis

As tension was increasing over Berlin, the USA also began to have problems closer to home. Cuba had long been the USA's economic ally, but revolution brought the communist threat to the USA's doorstep.

The Cuban Revolution in 1959 Worried the USA

1) Since 1952, Cuba had been ruled by Batista, a ruthless military dictator, who allowed American businessmen and the Mafia to make huge profits in a country where most people lived in poverty.

2) In 1956, a rebel called Fidel Castro began a guerrilla war. By 1959, he had enough support to take Cuba's capital, Havana, and successfully overthrew the government.

> In a 'guerrilla war', small military units use tactics like raids to fight a larger opponent.

3) This revolution worried the USA. The USA had a long economic history with Cuba. It owned half of Cuba's land and held most of the shares in all Cuban industries.

4) The USA felt it had a right to be involved in Cuba's affairs. But Cubans had grown to resent American influence in their country — they didn't feel like an independent state.

> The USA had occupied Cuba from 1898 to 1902. When Cuba became independent, the two countries maintained close economic ties.

The USA Accidentally pushed Castro Closer to the USSR

1) When Castro seized power in 1959, he nationalised US companies and increased taxes on goods imported from America. This angered the USA.

> 'Nationalisation' means taking a privately owned industry and placing it under public ownership.

2) Eisenhower was concerned that Castro's drive towards public ownership showed that he was moving towards communism.

3) He threatened to stop importing Cuban sugar. Sugar was Cuba's main source of wealth, and the USA was sure that Castro would back down.

4) Instead, Castro signed a trade agreement with the USSR — the USSR promised to buy all sugar exports. All remaining American property in Cuba was confiscated.

5) In January 1961, the USA severed all diplomatic relations with Cuba — the new US President John Kennedy no longer recognised Castro's government.

Comment and Analysis

Khrushchev wanted to help Castro, who was sympathetic towards communism. He also saw an opportunity to gain influence near US soil.

By 1961, Cuba had consolidated its ties with the USSR. As Cuba was only 100 miles from the USA, the communist threat had come dangerously close.

Rebels backed by the USA Invaded Cuba at the Bay of Pigs

Kennedy couldn't let a communist state emerge next to America — he intervened.

1) In 1961, Kennedy authorised an invasion of Cuba by anti-Castro rebels.

2) On 17th April 1961, the rebels landed in the Bay of Pigs, but they were easily defeated and the USA didn't help — it was a bit of a fiasco.

> Kennedy feared that communism might spread throughout Latin America, in countries such as Brazil, Bolivia and Venezuela.

3) Kennedy tried to hide US involvement in the invasion, but failed. The USA was humiliated, and had pushed Cuba even closer to the USSR. However, Kennedy was still determined to overthrow Castro.

> When Kennedy authorised the invasion, he had been acting on advice from military advisors who supported it and said it would be a success — Kennedy recognised that he had made a bad decision. He decided he would explore different options in the future with trusted advisors before deciding on a response. This new approach can be seen during one of the biggest crises of the Cold War — the Cuban Missile Crisis (p.40).

> **Tensions continued to grow...**
> - The invasion led Castro to decide that Cuba needed Soviet military assistance to defend itself. This would go on to spark the Cuban Missile Crisis in October 1962.
> - In December 1961, Castro publicly announced that he was a communist, confirming US fears.

The Cuban Missile Crisis

Cuba caused tension between the USA and the USSR. These activities will help you understand why.

Knowledge and Understanding

1) Describe what life was like in Cuba under Batista's rule.

2) How did Fidel Castro become leader of Cuba? Give as much detail as possible in your answer.

3) Copy and complete the table below, explaining why Cuba was important to the USA and the USSR.

Importance to the USA	Importance to the USSR

Thinking Historically

1) The flowchart below shows how the relationship between Cuba and the USA changed between 1959 and January 1961. Copy and complete the flowchart by adding the missing developments.

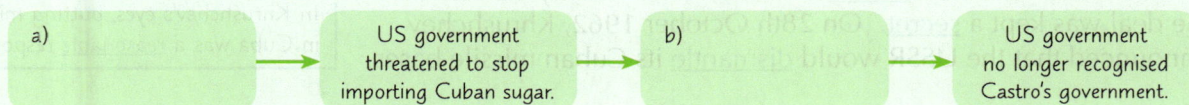

| a) | → | US government threatened to stop importing Cuban sugar. | → | b) | → | US government no longer recognised Castro's government. |

2) The USA acted against Cuba before they had any real evidence that Castro was a communist. Do you think this was the most important reason why Cuba and the USSR developed a closer relationship? Explain your answer.

3) Why did Kennedy intervene in Cuba in 1961? Describe how this intervention occurred.

4) Copy and complete the mind map below, listing the consequences of the Bay of Pigs invasion.

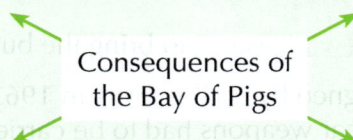

Consequences of the Bay of Pigs

EXAM TIP

The Bay of Pigs invasion wasn't Kennedy's finest moment...

Question 3 in the exam is about the causes and consequences of events, so make sure you know why key events happened and the impact that they had on international tensions.

Transformation of the Cold War

The Cuban Missile Crisis

Khrushchev agreed to help Castro and began to build nuclear missile sites in Cuba.

Khrushchev planned to put Nuclear Missiles in Cuba

1) In September 1961, Cuba asked the USSR for weapons to defend itself against further American intervention. By July 1962, Khrushchev had decided to put nuclear missiles in Cuba.

2) Although Khrushchev already had missiles that could reach the USA, missiles in Cuba would allow him to launch a nuclear attack on all of central and eastern USA with very little warning.

3) In October 1962, American U2 spy planes spotted that nuclear missile bases were being built in Cuba.

4) Some of Kennedy's advisors urged him to use military action to remove the missiles. Others promoted a less extreme response. Kennedy chose to avoid attacking Cuba — he ordered a naval blockade of the island instead. Soviet ships would be stopped and searched to prevent missiles being taken to Cuba.

5) As tensions rose, the USA made it clear that it would still take military action if necessary — bombers carrying nuclear bombs were put in the air and the USA prepared to invade Cuba. The world was on the brink of nuclear war.

6) Khrushchev sent Kennedy a letter, offering to remove the missiles from Cuba if the USA ended the naval blockade and pledged not to invade Cuba. Khrushchev then sent a second letter which had stronger demands — Soviet missile bases would only be dismantled if the USA removed its missiles from Turkey.

7) Kennedy continued to resist calls for military action. Instead, he decided to officially respond only to Khrushchev's first letter, accepting its terms. Kennedy also privately agreed to remove American missiles from Turkey — but this would only be done if the deal was kept a secret. On 28th October 1962, Khrushchev announced that the USSR would dismantle its Cuban missile bases.

Comment and Analysis

The USA had placed missiles in Turkey right next to the USSR in April 1962. In Khrushchev's eyes, putting missiles in Cuba was a reasonable response.

The crisis Significantly Altered the Course of the Cold War

The Cuban Missile Crisis was important — it showed the world how quickly a tense situation could become a catastrophe. In the short term, the powers made efforts to defuse tensions and improve communication.

- In 1963, a telephone 'hotline' was established between Washington and Moscow. This enabled the two superpowers to talk directly and more quickly in the event of a crisis.
- All nuclear missiles were removed from Cuba, and then from Turkey by April 1963.
- Kennedy emerged from the crisis as a hero who had stood up against the threat of communism.
- Khrushchev was discredited — he'd forced the USA to remove their missiles from Turkey, but agreed to keep the deal secret. In the eyes of the public he'd failed and he was removed from power in 1964.

In the long term, the crisis prompted new measures to bring the build up of nuclear weapons under control.

1) The Limited Test Ban Treaty was signed by both powers in 1963. It stated that all future tests of nuclear weapons had to be carried out underground to avoid polluting the air with nuclear radiation.

2) The Outer Space Treaty was drawn up in 1967. It forbade countries (including the USSR and the USA) from placing weapons of mass destruction in space.

3) The Nuclear Non-Proliferation Treaty came into force in 1970. Both superpowers agreed not to supply nuclear weapons or related technology to countries that didn't already have nuclear arms. The treaty also encouraged nuclear disarmament, but it allowed countries to use nuclear technology for peaceful purposes (e.g. energy).

The Cuban Missile Crisis was one of the most dangerous events in the Cold War, but it also contributed towards a period of 'détente' (see p.46).

The Cuban Missile Crisis

Use this page to help you learn about the causes, events and consequences of the Cuban Missile Crisis.

Knowledge and Understanding

1) Copy out the timeline below and use the information on pages 38 and 40 to fill in the events which took place on each date. Include as much detail as you can.

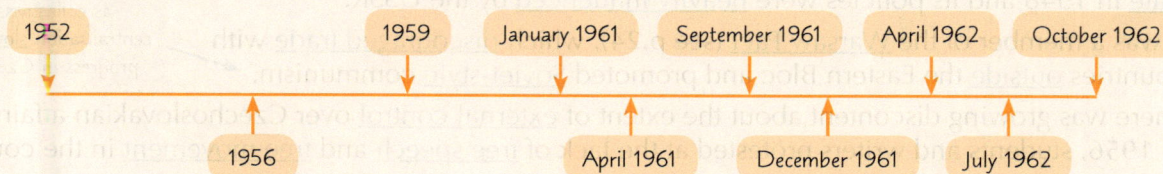

| 1952 | 1959 | January 1961 | September 1961 | April 1962 | October 1962 |

| 1956 | | April 1961 | December 1961 | July 1962 |

Thinking Historically

1) Copy and complete the mind map below, using the information on pages 38 and 40 to explain why each side felt they could claim victory in the Cuban Missile Crisis.

a) US 'victories' ← The Cuban Missile Crisis → b) Soviet 'victories'

2) Describe the positive changes that the superpowers made in each of the following areas after the Cuban Missile Crisis. Give as much information about the changes as you can.

a) Communication   b) Control of weapons

Source Analysis

The source below comes from a speech by President Kennedy. The speech was broadcast on US TV and radio on 22nd October 1962, the same day that Kennedy ordered a naval blockade of Cuba.

> For many years, both the Soviet Union and the United States... have deployed strategic nuclear weapons with great care, never upsetting the precarious* status quo** which insured that these weapons would not be used in the absence of some vital challenge. Our own strategic missiles have never been transferred to the territory of any other nation... But this secret, swift and extraordinary build-up of Communist missiles... is a deliberately provocative*** and unjustified change in the status quo which cannot be accepted by this country, if our courage and our commitments are ever to be trusted again by either friend or foe.

*delicate   **current situation   ***designed to provoke a reaction

1) Explain how useful this source would be for studying the causes of the Cuban Missile Crisis. You should write about the following features of the source in your answer:

The content of the source   The date of the source   The purpose of the source

---

EXAM TIP

A lot of good came out of the Cuban Missile Crisis...

It's important to learn the details of the treaties and measures introduced after the Missile Crisis. These developments help to show the impact of the crisis on relations between the superpowers.

The Prague Spring

In 1968, discontent within the Soviet Eastern Bloc stirred again. Czechoslovakia wanted more freedom from Moscow, and decided to move away from Soviet influence in a rebellion known as 'the Prague Spring'.

There was Opposition to Soviet Control in Czechoslovakia

1) Tension had been building in Czechoslovakia. It had become a communist state in 1948 and its policies were heavily influenced by the USSR.

2) It was a member of the Warsaw Pact (see p.24), which discouraged trade with countries outside the Eastern Bloc and promoted Soviet-style communism.

> Soviet policies such as collectivisation and centralisation slowed economic progress in Czechoslovakia.

3) There was growing discontent about the extent of external control over Czechoslovakian affairs. In 1956, students and writers protested at the lack of free speech and free movement in the country.

Dubcek wanted to Move Away from Soviet policies

1) In January 1968, Alexander Dubcek became the leader of the Communist Party in Czechoslovakia. Dubcek wanted Czechoslovakia to follow its own version of communism.

2) In April 1968, he introduced a series of reforms that went against Soviet-style communism.

Dubcek's Reforms

- Travel to the West was made available for all.
- The border with West Germany was re-opened.
- All industry became decentralised.
- Trade unions and workers were given more power.
- Freedom of speech and opposition parties were allowed.

> Decentralisation meant that companies were no longer controlled by Communist Party officials — workers and local authorities were given more power.

3) Many of the reforms were aimed at improving the performance of Czechoslovakia's economy — partly by developing closer relations with the West.

4) This worried the USSR — it didn't want any Western involvement in its Eastern Bloc.

5) Even though some reforms moved away from Soviet policy, Dubcek was still a communist. He promised that Czechoslovakia would stay in the Warsaw Pact and remain a loyal ally to Moscow.

6) For four months, Dubcek's new policies were tolerated by the USSR, and Czechoslovakia enjoyed relative freedom. This period is known as the 'Prague Spring'.

The USSR was Under Pressure to Intervene

1) The USSR grew increasingly concerned about Dubcek's reforms. Dubcek promised he was still loyal to Moscow, but his new policies meant that the USSR had less control over Czechoslovakia.

2) The leader of the USSR, Leonid Brezhnev, was worried that Dubcek's reforms could lead to a rejection of communism in the Eastern Bloc and in the USSR itself. If Czechoslovakia pulled away, other satellite states might follow.

Events in August 1968 triggered a Soviet response...

- President Tito of Yugoslavia visited Prague. Yugoslavia had refused to sign the Warsaw Pact and had never accepted the USSR's version of communism. The trip was an ominous sign to Brezhnev that Czechoslovakia was no longer loyal to the USSR.
- The USSR received a letter from communists in Czechoslovakia, asking for help.

The Prague Spring

These activities will help you understand the events that led to the Prague Spring and the USSR's response.

Knowledge and Understanding

1) Describe the relationship between Czechoslovakia and the USSR before 1968.

2) What was the Prague Spring?

3) Copy and complete the mind map below, adding all the reforms introduced by Dubcek in 1968.

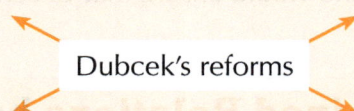

Dubcek's reforms

4) Why did Dubcek introduce these reforms?

5) How did Dubcek seek to reassure the USSR that he did not intend to break away from its control?

Thinking Historically

1) Explain why each of the following factors encouraged the USSR to intervene in Czechoslovakia:

a) The Eastern Bloc   b) President Tito   c) Czechoslovakian communists

Source Analysis

The source on the right is a cartoon produced in Britain in July 1968. The man in the cartoon is Alexander Dubcek.

1) Imagine you are using this source for an investigation into attitudes towards the Prague Spring. Explain how each feature of the source listed below affects its usefulness for your investigation.

a) Content   b) Date   c) Where it was produced

STALIN 1879-1953

© The Times / News Licensing

Dubcek wanted to reform Czechoslovakia peacefully...

EXAM TIP

The Prague Spring shows how important the USSR's relationship with its satellite states was during the Cold War — the USSR couldn't afford to let Czechoslovakia pull away completely.

Transformation of the Cold War

The Prague Spring

In August 1968, the USSR decided to intervene militarily. This led to a new pro-Soviet leader in power and Czechoslovakia returned to Soviet-style communism.

The USSR Invaded Czechoslovakia in August 1968

1) On 21st August 1968 500,000 Soviet troops invaded Czechoslovakia.

2) The Czechoslovakians responded with non-violent demonstrations — people took to the streets with anti-invasion banners, and in January 1969 a student burned himself alive in the street in protest.

> Czechoslovakia was keen to avoid the violence that erupted in the 1956 Hungarian Uprising (see p.28).

3) In April 1969, Dubcek was forcibly removed from office, and replaced with Gustav Husak. Husak was loyal to Soviet-style communism, and would ensure that Czechoslovakia remained close with the USSR.

The Soviet invasion Strained Relations between East and West

1) The Soviet invasion of Czechoslovakia showed the West that Brezhnev was determined to keep control of the USSR's satellite states — he was willing to use force to uphold communism and to keep the anti-Western alliance strong.

2) The West criticised the USSR, but took little action against them.

> The West was wary of taking action against the USSR. The Prague Spring occurred at a time when the Cold War had thawed slightly. Nobody wanted to re-ignite tensions.

- The USA and many other Western countries condemned the Soviet action but didn't intervene. They were worried about interfering within the USSR's sphere of influence.
- American President Lyndon B. Johnson cancelled a summit meeting with Brezhnev in response to the USSR's actions.
- The UN denounced the invasion and proposed a draft resolution requesting the withdrawal of Soviet troops from Czechoslovakia. This was vetoed (rejected) by the USSR.
- Communist parties in the West criticised Brezhnev's reaction and sought to distance themselves from Soviet influence.

Warsaw Pact forces enter Prague in August 1968.

© Mary Evans / Iberfoto

3) The invasion also damaged relations between the USSR and some of the Eastern Bloc countries, who felt threatened by the Soviet response. Romania and Albania both refused to participate in the invasion, and Albania withdrew from the Warsaw Pact shortly afterwards. The invasion also created long-lasting resentment towards the USSR in Czechoslovakia.

The Brezhnev Doctrine worried other communist countries

1) After the invasion, Brezhnev announced that in future the USSR would act to protect communism in any country where it was under threat. This policy became known as the Brezhnev Doctrine.

2) The Brezhnev Doctrine was important because it strengthened the USSR's control over its satellite states.

3) It also sent a message to the Eastern Bloc that giving up communism or making reforms to Soviet policy wasn't an option — the USSR would respond with force.

> However, the Brezhnev Doctrine also led the US government to believe that the USSR was more concerned with keeping its existing territory than with expanding further. In fact, it provided evidence for US politicians who argued that American troops were no longer needed in Europe.

4) Mao feared that the Soviets could use the Brezhnev Doctrine to justify an invasion of China — relations between China and the USSR had been worsening since the late 1950s.

5) The relationship between America and the Soviet Union continued to be strained — the Brezhnev Doctrine made it clear that the Cold War wasn't over.

The Prague Spring

Use these activities to test your understanding of the invasion of Czechoslovakia and the Brezhnev Doctrine.

Knowledge and Understanding

1) The flowchart below shows the stages in the USSR's intervention in Czechoslovakia. Copy and complete the flowchart, describing what happened at each stage.

a) Invasion of Czechoslovakia → b) Czechoslovakian response → c) Replacement of Dubcek

2) How did the following countries and groups react to the invasion of Czechoslovakia?

a) Western countries   b) The UN   c) Communist parties in the West   d) The Eastern Bloc

3) What was the Brezhnev Doctrine?

Source Analysis

Source A

The weakening of any of the links in the world system of socialism* directly affects all the socialist countries, which cannot look indifferently** upon this... Czechoslovakia's detachment from the socialist community, would have come into conflict with its own vital interests and would have been detrimental*** to the other socialist states... the USSR and the other socialist states had to act decisively and they did act against the antisocialist forces in Czechoslovakia.

*'socialism' is used in this extract to mean communism
**without interest   ***harmful

Source A is an extract from a speech made by Brezhnev in November 1968.

Source B

Source B is a photograph of protestors outside the Soviet Trade Exhibition in London in August 1968.

1) Imagine you are using Source A for an investigation into attitudes towards the Soviet invasion of Czechoslovakia. Explain how the features below affect its usefulness for your investigation.

a) Author   b) Purpose   c) Date   d) Content

2) Explain why the content and date of Source B might make it useful for the same investigation.

3) Why do you think the sources might be useful as a pair for investigating attitudes towards the Soviet invasion of Czechoslovakia? Explain your answer.

EXAM TIP

The Brezhnev Doctrine kept the Eastern Bloc loyal...

Question 4 in the exam could ask you to analyse the main cause of a development. Making a mind map is a great way to make sure you can remember what all the different causes are.

Détente

In the 1970s there was a period of 'détente' — an easing in tension between the two superpowers.

Tensions still Existed between the superpowers Before Détente

The relationship between the USA and the USSR was still strained by the 1970s for a variety of reasons:

- The USA was critical of the USSR for its record on human rights. Soviet leaders denied citizens religious and political freedoms, as well as freedom of speech, and the right to emigrate.
- Suspicion and distrust between the two powers had been fuelled by developments such as America's increasing involvement in Vietnam (p.20), and the USSR's intervention in the Prague Spring (p.44).

The policy of Détente was Practical

Despite the sources of tension that still existed between the superpowers, they both realised the importance of avoiding conflict. In an attempt to improve relations, the USA and the USSR followed a policy of détente.

1) The 1960s were marked by crises, such as in Berlin (p.34 and p.36) and Cuba (p.38 and p 40), which were some of the most tense moments in the Cold War. Both powers wanted to avoid other near misses.

2) Boosting military power hadn't reduced tensions. Both countries saw that a new strategy was needed.

3) The USA and the USSR were struggling financially. The US economy was suffering as a result of rising inflation and the cost of the Vietnam War, while the USSR was worried about falling living standards in the Eastern Bloc. As a result, both powers were keen to reduce their military spending — the arms race was extremely expensive. Both powers also saw the economic advantages of increasing trade with each other.

> In 1970, riots over high living costs broke out in Poland.

4) China was becoming more powerful, and its alliance with the Soviet Union had weakened. The USA took this opportunity to improve relations with China. The Soviets feared that an alliance between China and the USA would develop — to avoid this, the USSR became more open to co-operating with America.

The Superpowers agreed to Reduce Arms and Co-operate

1) US President Richard Nixon and Soviet Leader Leonid Brezhnev played an important role in reducing tension. Both leaders had reasons for wanting to improve relations:
   - Nixon needed a foreign policy success to draw attention away from criticism he was facing in the USA for the Vietnam War.
   - Brezhnev was worried by a visit Nixon made to China in February 1972 — he wanted to make sure that the USA and China wouldn't join forces against the USSR.

> Nixon became the first US president to visit Moscow, and only the second to visit the USSR.

2) In May 1972, Nixon visited Moscow. The two leaders signed seven agreements, covering arms control, space exploration, trade and other areas. The most important of these was the First Strategic Arms Limitation Treaty, known as SALT 1. This treaty aimed to slow down the arms race and ease tensions.

- SALT 1 limited the number of ABMs (anti-ballistic missiles) each country could have and placed a temporary limit on the numbers of ICBMs (Intercontinental Ballistic Missiles) on both sides.
- ABMs were designed to intercept incoming missiles and had the potential to upset the delicate 'nuclear balance' between the USSR and the USA.

> If one side could use ABMs to destroy the other side's missiles, then the threat of retaliation would be gone. The side with ABMs could launch a first strike and then just destroy the missiles that were fired back towards it.

Comment and Analysis

By limiting the number of ABMs each country could have, SALT 1 reduced the likelihood of one country holding an advantage over the other.

3) Despite the progress made by 1972, détente didn't lead to the end of the Cold War. Tensions between America and the Soviet Union reignited in 1979, and the Cold War didn't end until 1991.

Détente

The activities on this page will help to improve your understanding of why tensions eased in the 1970s.

Knowledge and Understanding

1) Write a definition for the term 'détente'.

2) Explain why there was still tension between the USA and the USSR in the 1970s. Give as much detail as you can.

3) Explain why each of the following leaders wanted to improve relations between the USA and the USSR when they met in May 1972:

   a) Richard Nixon   b) Leonid Brezhnev

4) Explain what ABMs are and why they threatened to upset the 'nuclear balance' between the USA and the USSR.

5) Copy and complete the mind map below about SALT 1.

   a) What was its aim? ← SALT 1 → c) How did it reduce tensions?

   b) What was agreed?

Thinking Historically

1) 'The crises that occurred in the 1960s were the main reason why there was a period of détente in the 1970s.' Use the table below to help you structure each paragraph of an essay that explains how far you agree with the statement above.

Point	Evidence	Why evidence supports point
In 1962, the USA and USSR came close to nuclear war. They wanted to avoid this happening again, and this contributed to détente.	After the USSR moved missiles to Cuba, the USA put bombers carrying nuclear bombs in the air and prepared to invade Cuba. The situation was resolved, but both sides wanted to avoid other near misses.	Crises like the Cuban Missile Crisis showed how important it was for the USA and the USSR to improve relations. Building up military strength hadn't reduced tensions so a policy of détente was followed in the 1970s instead.

Add three rows to the table to structure three more paragraphs.

Think about whether there are any links between different reasons.

You can use evidence from across this section to back up your points.

They should have just put each other in détente-ion...

EXAM TIP

In the exam, it's important to spend a few minutes planning your answers to longer questions before you start writing. This will help you to keep your answers focused and organised.

Transformation of the Cold War

Worked Exam-Style Question

Have a look at this sample answer and the comments to help you tackle the 16-mark question in the exam.

'The USA was mainly responsible for tensions between the superpowers in the 1960s.'

Explain how far you agree with this statement.   [16 marks]

For questions like this in the exam, 4 extra marks will be available for spelling, punctuation, grammar and using specialist terms.

The actions of the USA in the 1960s were an important cause of tension between the superpowers. However, tension was also caused by the USSR's actions, and it would not be fair to blame tensions in the 1960s only on the USA. In reality, the most important reason for tension in the 1960s was the way that the two superpowers provoked each other into taking aggressive actions as both powers tried to spread their own ideology and increase their influence.

This introduction gives a basic answer to the question.

The USA played an important role in causing tension between the superpowers in the 1960s. One example where this can be seen is America's aggressive approach to stopping the spread of communism in Vietnam. From 1965, the USA began sending troops to Vietnam to try to defeat the Vietcong and stop Vietnam from becoming a communist country. This caused tension between the two superpowers because the USSR viewed these actions as aggressive and criticised the USA. Another important way the USA contributed to tensions between the superpowers was when they were caught spying on the Soviets in May 1960. When the Soviets shot down a U2 American spy plane, Eisenhower lied by denying that it was a spy plane, and then refused to apologise when the USSR produced the pilot and the plane's wreckage as evidence. This angered Khrushchev, and caused him to walk out of the Paris Peace Summit days later, which meant that an opportunity to improve relations had been lost.

This directly addresses the factor given in the question.

Explain how each factor caused tensions.

However, the actions of the USSR also created tension between the superpowers in the 1960s. For example, the USSR built the Berlin Wall in 1961, which prevented anyone from leaving East Berlin to go to West Berlin. This increased tension because the USA condemned this aggressive Soviet behaviour. The wall also brought the two sides close to conflict at Checkpoint Charlie, when US and Soviet tanks were involved in a stand-off over a border dispute. Similarly, the USSR's invasion of Czechoslovakia in 1968 was a major cause of tension between the superpowers. The USSR invaded Czechoslovakia and replaced its leader, Dubcek, after he began introducing reforms that went against Soviet-style communism. The invasion caused tension between the superpowers because it showed the West that the Soviets were still willing to use force to keep control of the USSR's sphere

This is bringing in a different factor to explain tensions. Even if you agree with the statement, it's important to look at other factors to show you've considered alternative arguments.

Use accurate details from your own knowledge to back up your points.

Worked Exam-Style Question

Try to link back to the question at the end of every paragraph.

of influence and maintain a strong anti-western alliance. This suggests that the USSR was just as responsible as the USA for causing tensions in the 1960s by acting aggressively.

However, even when it seemed that one country was acting more aggressively than the other, the main reason for tensions was often that the two countries provoked each other. For example, the USA acted aggressively in Vietnam because the US government had seen the USSR's support for communism in China and Korea and was worried that the Soviets were plotting to spread communism to other Asian countries, such as Vietnam. The USSR also gave aid to communist North Vietnam during the Vietnam War, which would have encouraged American fears that the USSR wanted to turn Vietnam into a fully communist country. Therefore, the USSR played an important role in fuelling American feelings of fear and suspicion over Vietnam.

This makes links between different factors by stating that the USA and the USSR influenced each other's actions.

This gives another example to back up the argument.

Similarly, both sides contributed to escalating tensions in Berlin in the 1960s. Although it was the USSR who built the Berlin Wall, the USA provoked them into taking this action by helping to strengthen West Germany's economy, while East Germany remained weak under the Soviets. This made the USSR feel threatened because they believed that the USA was trying to make communism look weak and draw the satellite states away from the USSR. The USSR's decision to build the Berlin Wall, therefore, was an attempt to protect their sphere of influence from what they saw as US interference.

Start a new paragraph every time you introduce a new point.

The clearest example of the two superpowers provoking each other was the Cuban Missile Crisis. The USSR contributed to tensions by developing its links with Cuba. This worried the USA because it did not want a Soviet-backed communist country so close to US soil. However, the USA escalated tensions by authorising an invasion of Cuba by anti-Castro rebels at the Bay of Pigs in April 1961. To protect Cuba from American aggression, the USSR decided to build missile bases in Cuba in July 1962. When America discovered these bases in October 1962, the two sides came close to nuclear war. However, Khrushchev believed the decision to put missiles on Cuba was reasonable because the USA had put missiles in Turkey, right next to the USSR, in April 1962. Therefore, the Cuban Missile Crisis, one of the biggest crises of the 1960s, was caused by the USA and the USSR responding to each other's actions.

Include specific dates to show you have a good knowledge of the period.

Summarise your argument in your conclusion.

Overall, although the USA was responsible for causing tension in the 1960s over issues such as Vietnam and the U2 incident, the USSR also contributed to tensions in places like Berlin and Czechoslovakia. However, the main reason for tension between the powers in the 1960s was the fact that the USA and the USSR constantly provoked each other into taking aggressive actions that escalated the tension between them.

Make sure you clearly state your opinion in the conclusion.

Exam-Style Questions

Try your hand at these exam-style questions about some of the biggest crises of the Cold War.

Source A

A cartoon published in 1967. It was drawn by Hungarian artist Victor Vashi, who spent time in a Soviet prison camp in the 1940s.

The cartoon shows a man whose body is divided in half by the Berlin Wall.

Source B

A 1961 cartoon by the Danish artist Herluf Bidstrup, which refers to the Bay of Pigs invasion in Cuba. Bidstrup was a communist, and his work was popular in the Soviet Union

In the cartoon, the figure with the knife represents the USA. 'CCCP' is a Russian abbreviation for the Soviet Union.

Exam-Style Questions

Source C

An extract from a letter written by Nikita Khrushchev to John F. Kennedy on 22nd April 1961. Khrushchev is writing about the Bay of Pigs invasion.

> Mr. President, I have received your reply of April 18. You write that the United States intends no military intervention in Cuba. But numerous facts known to the whole world — and to the Government of the United States, of course, better than to any one else — speak differently. Despite all assurances* to the contrary, it has now been proved beyond doubt that it was precisely the United States which prepared the intervention, financed its arming and transported the gangs of mercenaries** that invaded the territory of Cuba. United States armed forces also took a direct part in the accomplishment of the gangster attack upon Cuba. American bombers and fighters supported the operations of the mercenaries who landed on Cuban territory, and participated in the military operations against the armed forces of the lawful Government and people of Cuba. Such are the facts. They bear witness to direct United States participation in the armed aggression against Cuba.

*promises   **paid soldiers

Exam-Style Questions

1) How can you tell that Source A is critical of the Soviet Union?
   Use Source A and your own knowledge to explain your answer.   [4 marks]

2) Look at Source B and Source C. How useful would these sources be to a historian studying attitudes towards the Bay of Pigs invasion?
   Use both sources and your own knowledge to explain your answer.   [12 marks]

3) Give an account of how the USSR's invasion of Czechoslovakia caused international tensions.   [8 marks]

4) 'The construction of the Berlin Wall was the main reason for Cold War tensions in the 1960s.'

   Explain how far you agree with this statement.   [16 marks]

> For the 16-mark question in the exam, 4 extra marks will be available for spelling, punctuation, grammar and using specialist terminology.

Answers

The Origins of the Cold War

Page 7 — The End of the Second World War

Knowledge and Understanding

1 a) • Politics — The USA had a democratically elected government.
   - Economy — The US economy was based on private ownership of property, free competition and forces of supply and demand.
   - Human rights — The USA believed in personal rights and freedoms, such as freedom of speech.

  b) • Politics — The USSR was a single-party state.
   - Economy — The economy was controlled by the government and there was no private ownership of property.
   - Human rights — The state decided what rights its citizens had, and it could take these rights away. Freedom of speech was restricted.

2   The USA disliked the USSR's ideology because communism aimed at world revolution, so the USA saw it as a danger to democracy and American freedoms. The USSR disliked the USA's ideology because it believed that capitalism led to the exploitation of workers and the unfair distribution of wealth.

3 a) Stalin wanted to gain influence over Eastern European countries. He thought they would help protect the USSR against attacks that he feared might come from the West.

  b) Roosevelt wanted to create the United Nations, a peacekeeping force that would allow the USA to step back from Europe. He also wanted to co-operate with

Stalin, partly to make sure that Stalin gave the USA support against Japan.

  c) Churchill wanted to preserve Britain's global power and limit the influence of the USSR in Europe. He also wanted Germany to be politically and economically stable so there wouldn't be any more unrest there.

4 a) • Eastern Europe would become the USSR's 'sphere of influence'.
   - Liberated Eastern European countries would hold free elections.
   - Germany and Berlin would each be divided into four zones. The USA, the USSR, Britain and France would control one zone each.
   - The United Nations would be set up to replace the failed League of Nations.

  b) • The new boundaries of Poland were decided.
   - It was confirmed that Germany and Berlin would be divided into zones and split between the Allies.

Thinking Historically

1 a) Roosevelt is replaced by Truman, who is more suspicious of the USSR and is less willing to compromise. Truman wants to limit the USSR's 'sphere of influence' in Eastern Europe, however Stalin fears attacks from the West and believes a sphere of influence would help protect the Soviet Union. This makes it harder for the two sides to work together.

  b) The USA sees this as a violation of the Yalta agreement on free elections. This damages the relationship between the USA and the USSR because it makes the USA trust Stalin even less than before.

2 Here are some points your answer may include:
- During World War Two, the members of the Grand Alliance were fighting a common enemy, so they put aside their differences and worked together to defeat the Nazis. Once the war was over, the relationship began to break down as tensions developed between the USA and the USSR.
- After the death of President Roosevelt, the USA was led by Truman. This had a negative impact on the relationship between the members of the Grand Alliance because Truman was more suspicious of the USSR and less prepared to compromise.
- The agreements made at Yalta caused conflict when they were put into practice. When Stalin began installing a pro-communist government in Poland after Yalta, the USA was alarmed because this went against the agreement made at Yalta that countries in Eastern Europe would have free elections. However, Stalin would have considered this acceptable because at Yalta the Allies had agreed to the USSR having a 'sphere of influence' in Eastern Europe. These differing perspectives created tension between the two sides.
- Disagreements about the future of Germany increased tension between the members of the Grand Alliance. Stalin wanted to keep Germany weak, but Truman was worried this would make Germany vulnerable to Soviet expansion.
- The different ideologies of the USA and the USSR made it difficult for them to trust each other. The USA felt threatened by the USSR's aim of world revolution, and the USSR feared that the USA would achieve worldwide influence.

Page 9 — The Two Superpowers
Knowledge and Understanding
1 The USA dropped two atom bombs on Japan in August 1945, destroying the cities of Hiroshima and Nagasaki.
2 Any four from: Poland, Hungary, Romania, Bulgaria, Yugoslavia, Albania.
3 a) Stalin installed a pro-Soviet 'puppet' government in Czechoslovakia. For a while, it seemed like Czechoslovakia might remain democratic. However, the Communist Party seized power in February 1948 when it seemed likely to lose ground in the next election.
  b) East Germany was given to the USSR when Germany was divided between the Allies at Yalta. The USSR installed a communist government there. Stalin did this by telling a group of German communists to join with the German Social Democratic Party to form the Socialist Unity Party of Germany. The communists then removed the original members of the SPD and took control.
4 a) The Cold War describes the situation that developed between the USA and the USSR after the Second World War, where there were increasing tensions between the two countries but there was no direct fighting between them.
  b) The Iron Curtain was how Winston Churchill described the divide between the communist countries of Eastern Europe and the capitalist, pro-USA countries of Western Europe.
Thinking Historically
1 • The development of the atom bomb meant that the USA no longer needed the USSR's assistance to defeat Japan, and so they bypassed a military alliance with the Soviets. The USA then refused to let the Soviets occupy Japan, which showed that it did not trust the USSR. This damaged the relationship between the two countries,

creating tension between them.
- The USA had kept the exact nature of the atom bomb a secret from the USSR at Potsdam in July 1945. This made Stalin more suspicious of the West.
- Stalin saw the development of the atom bomb as an attempt to intimidate the USSR.
- Stalin was angry that the USA had managed to surpass Soviet technology by developing nuclear weapons first.
- The development of the atom bomb increased the military rivalry between the two countries as the USSR sped up development of its own atom bomb. This started an arms race between the two countries.

2 Stalin installed pro-Soviet 'puppet' governments in many of the countries of Eastern Europe between 1945 and 1948. This increased tensions between the USSR and the West because Stalin had agreed at Yalta that the liberated Eastern European countries would hold free elections, so he was breaking his promise. It also increased tensions because it meant that these Eastern European countries were now under the influence of the USSR, and this worried Western countries, who were concerned by the growing power of the USSR and the spread of communism.

3 Churchill's 'Iron Curtain' speech shows how difficult relations were between the West and the USSR after the Second World War. The speech demonstrates that the Grand Alliance had broken down, as Britain and the USA no longer viewed the USSR as an ally. Instead, the West now viewed the USSR as a threat.

Page 11 — Mutual Suspicion
Knowledge and Understanding
1 a) The USA pledged to provide diplomatic, military or financial support to any country that was threatened by a communist takeover. The US government introduced this policy because it believed that the USA had a duty to help those who were facing pressure from communist forces. The USA believed that intervention was the only way to maintain world peace and American security.
  b) The USA promised $17 billion of aid to European countries to help them rebuild their economies. The US government hoped that the Marshall Plan would contain communism and help ease suffering in Europe. Countries that received aid were expected to co-operate with the USA and to import American goods. This would create markets for US goods in Europe, which would benefit the US economy.
2 Stalin felt threatened by the Truman Doctrine and reacted by strengthening and uniting his allies. He set up Cominform in 1947, which brought together all European communist parties and put them under the control of the USSR. Stalin also ordered the USSR's satellite states to reject Marshall Plan aid, and set up Comecon in 1949 as an alternative. Comecon placed industry and agriculture under state control and offered satellite states economic aid.
3 Unlike other countries in Eastern Europe, Yugoslavia challenged Soviet domination. It had freed itself from the Nazis without the Red Army's assistance. This meant that it owed less loyalty to the USSR and was more independent. As a result, Yugoslavia was more open to the West and President Tito often refused to obey Stalin, causing tension between the two leaders. In June 1948, Yugoslavia was expelled from Cominform and the country became an independent communist state. It later received economic aid from the USA.

Answers

Source Analysis

1 a) The source is a cartoon that was produced in the USA. This makes it useful for the investigation, because it might reflect some of the views that the American public had about the Marshall Plan.

   b) The source was produced in 1947, which makes it useful for the investigation because the Marshall Plan was announced in June 1947. This means that the source might reflect Americans' attitudes to the Marshall Plan around the time it was introduced.

   c) The content of the source is useful because it suggests that Americans thought the Marshall Plan would help to 'rescue' Europe from communism. In the cartoon, Europe is able to 'climb away' from communism by using the Marshall Plan as a rope. This suggests that some Americans were supportive of the Marshall Plan because it aimed to stop communism from spreading.

2 • Source B was written jointly by the communist parties of nine European countries. This makes it useful for the investigation, because it shows what communist party members across Europe thought about the Marshall Plan. These parties came together to make Cominform, which put them under the control of the USSR. This makes the source useful in showing the attitudes of people who held anti-capitalist and pro-Soviet views.

   • The source was written in October 1947, a few months after the Marshall Plan was announced in June. This makes the source useful for the investigation because it shows how communist parties across Europe reacted to the Marshall Plan shortly after it was announced.

   • The content of the source is useful because it shows that communists in Europe believed that the Marshall Plan was a cover for the USA's attempts to increase their influence in Europe. The source argues that the Marshall Plan is part of the USA's 'general world plan of political expansion'.

3 The sources might be useful as a pair because they show the different attitudes that people on each side of the Cold War had towards the Marshall Plan. Source A shows the attitude of some Americans, whereas Source B shows the opinions of European communist party members. Therefore, the two sources highlight the differences in perspective on the opposite sides of the Cold War.

Page 13 — The Berlin Crisis

Thinking Historically

1 a) West Berlin's strong capitalist economy embarrassed the USSR and made communism look weak.

   b) West Berlin faced shortages of food and other essential items, such as fuel, water and medicine. Travel to and from Berlin was also severely restricted. Even after the Western powers began airlifting supplies to West Berlin, food and electricity were rationed, and shortages of coal meant that many people struggled to heat their homes.

2 a) The Berlin crisis gave the USA a huge propaganda victory over the USSR. During the crisis, the USA appeared strong and committed to protecting freedom from Soviet aggression, while Stalin was humiliated.

   b) Many Germans respected the USA for its actions during the crisis. They now viewed the Americans as defenders of the German people and not just an occupying force.

   c) The USSR's reputation in Europe was severely damaged because of the suffering caused by the blockade.

   d) It became clear that the two superpowers wouldn't come to an agreement over Berlin and that Germany would remain divided. In 1949, two separate states were formed — West Germany and East Germany.

Source Analysis

1 a) The birds represent the Western planes bringing essential supplies to the people of West Berlin during the Soviet blockade. This is critical of the USSR because it suggests that the USSR caused suffering in West Berlin by denying the people access to basic items, such as coal and food. The people of West Berlin had to rely on Western planes to bring them these supplies instead.

   b) Storks are associated with bringing new life, which reflects that Western planes brought supplies to the West Berliners, enabling West Berlin and its people to continue to survive. This is critical of the USSR because it praises the West for rescuing West Berlin and its people from Stalin, who is causing them harm.

   c) The fact that Stalin is watching on with a gun reflects that the planes airlifting supplies to West Berlin could have been shot down at any moment by the USSR. This is critical of the USSR because it suggests that Stalin is an aggressor who wants to stop the supply of food and goods reaching the people of West Berlin.

Pages 16-17 — Exam-Style Questions

1 This question is level marked. How to grade your answer:

Level 1 1-2 marks	The answer gives a basic analysis of relevant features of the source's content and/or provenance. It is supported by simple background knowledge.
Level 2 3-4 marks	The answer gives a more developed analysis of relevant features of the source's content and/or provenance. It is supported by relevant background knowledge.

Here are some points your answer may include:

   • We know that Source A is critical of the West, because it suggests that the West used economic aid to control other countries. The cartoon's caption claims that the West gave economic aid to Tito, and in return expected him to pretend that Yugoslavia had 'independence'. The cartoon is therefore suggesting that Yugoslavia is actually under the influence of the West and that the West is asking Yugoslavia to pretend that it isn't. This could be in response to the fact that Tito accepted economic aid from the USA after Stalin expelled Yugoslavia from Cominform in June 1948. The Soviets were critical of this sort of economic involvement from the USA in Europe, believing that it was a way for the USA to gain power there and encourage Eastern European states to reject communism. The source reflects this Soviet attitude to US economic aid in Europe, which is how we can tell it is critical of the West.

   • We know that the cartoon is critical of the West because it accuses the West of bullying Yugoslavia. It does this by portraying Tito, the leader of Yugoslavia, as a tiny figure, and the West as large figures who surround Tito and seem to dominate him. This reflects the USSR's critical view that the West wanted to spread their influence and control over European countries, such as Yugoslavia, and undermine the USSR's sphere of influence. We know that the source is critical of the West, therefore, because it reflects the attitudes of the USSR by portraying the West as an oppressive and intimidating force.

Answers

2 This question is level marked. How to grade your answer:

Level 1 1-3 marks	The answer shows a limited understanding of one or both sources and gives a basic analysis of them.
Level 2 4-6 marks	The answer gives a simple evaluation of one or both sources based on their content and/or provenance.
Level 3 7-9 marks	The answer evaluates the content and/or provenance of both sources in more detail to make judgements about their usefulness.
Level 4 10-12 marks	The answer evaluates the content and provenance of both sources to make a developed judgement about their usefulness. The answer is supported with relevant background knowledge.

Here are some points your answer may include:

- Source B is useful to a historian studying attitudes towards America's possession of the atom bomb, because it shows that the USA saw its nuclear weapons as a positive addition to its military force. This can be seen in the way that Truman describes how the atom bomb would bring a 'revolutionary increase in destruction' to the 'growing power' of the US armed forces, and how 'even more powerful' bombs were in development. This source was produced in 1945, a time when tensions between the USA and the USSR were rising, so America would have seen the military advantage which their nuclear weapons gave them as a positive thing.

- Source B is also useful because it shows that Truman recognised the danger of nuclear weapons, but believed that America was capable of handling the responsibility of being the world's only nuclear power. Truman acknowledges that the atom bomb poses the 'danger of sudden destruction', but also states that America would consider ways to both 'control the production and use of atomic power', and use nuclear weapons for the 'maintenance of world peace'. The source is useful to a historian, therefore, because it reveals that the USA considered it necessary to show the world that it was a responsible country, and that its possession of nuclear weapons was a force for good. This may have been because America wanted to project a positive image of itself to the world at a time when rivalry was growing between it and the Soviet Union.

- However, Source B's usefulness is limited because it doesn't explicitly refer to the other reasons why America viewed its possession of the bomb positively. One of these reasons is that being the only nuclear power in the world boosted the USA's power and status and gave it a significant advantage over the USSR. While Truman states that the USA will not reveal details about the 'production or all the military applications' of the bomb in the interest of safety, it is also true that the USA knew that it benefitted from being the only nuclear power in the world. It is unlikely that the president would openly discuss this issue in a public statement, so the source doesn't offer a full picture of America's attitude towards owning the bomb, which limits its usefulness.

- Source C is useful because it shows that the USSR viewed America's possession of nuclear weapons in a much more negative light. Produced by the Soviet Union, the poster presents the USA as a small, hunched, villainous figure carrying a bomb. The poster also shows the USA being scolded by a strong and authoritative Soviet figure. The source is useful therefore, because it suggests that the Soviet Union viewed America's development and use of the atom bomb as reckless and wrong. It shows that the Soviets believed they had a rational and sensible approach to nuclear weapons, while they saw the USA as irresponsible and childish.

- Source C's usefulness is limited, however, because it doesn't reflect other reasons why the USSR viewed America's possession of the atom bomb negatively. The Soviets were actually angry that American technology had managed to surpass their own. Stalin felt greatly threatened by the USA's nuclear advantage, and increased Soviet efforts to develop nuclear weapons immediately after the US bombing of Japan. Source C doesn't address these issues because it is a propaganda poster designed to reflect the Soviets in a positive way. This source, therefore, wouldn't acknowledge the USSR's vulnerability or its attempt to match the USA's nuclear power, which limits its usefulness to a historian studying attitudes towards America's possession of the atom bomb.

- The sources are particularly useful when they are taken together, as they highlight the differences between the attitudes of the USA and the USSR towards America's possession of the atom bomb. The sources show that while America viewed its nuclear advantage positively, the USSR discredited its possession of the atom bomb by portraying the USA as irresponsible and dangerous. This reflects how America's use of atom bombs in Japan in 1945 intensified the rivalry between the two powers.

3 This question is level marked. How to grade your answer:

Level 1 1-2 marks	The answer gives a basic analysis of causes and/or consequences. It lacks any clear organisation and shows limited relevant background knowledge.
Level 2 3-4 marks	The answer gives a simple analysis of causes and/or consequences. It has some organisation and it shows some relevant background knowledge.
Level 3 5-6 marks	The answer gives a more developed analysis of causes and/or consequences. It is well organised and shows a range of accurate and relevant background knowledge.
Level 4 7-8 marks	The answer gives a highly developed analysis of causes and/or consequences. It is very well organised and demonstrates a range of accurate and detailed background knowledge that is relevant to the question.

Here are some points your answer may include:

- The Berlin Crisis increased Cold War tensions by showing that the USSR was not afraid to take direct action against the West. In an attempt to make the Western powers leave West Berlin, Stalin cut off access to that part of the city in 1948 by blocking all road, rail and canal links. Stalin's decision to begin this blockade increased Cold War tensions because it represented an escalation towards more forceful opposition to the USA.

- Tensions rose further during the Berlin Crisis when the West refused to retreat from the city. Instead, America responded to the blockade by flying supplies into West Berlin, and they continued this Airlift for 318 days. This caused Cold War tensions between the East and the West to rise, because it showed that the USA was committed to its policy of containment and would not allow the USSR to expand its sphere of influence over the whole of Berlin.

- The Berlin Crisis increased Cold War tensions because

56

Answers

it highlighted the USA's nuclear superiority to the Soviet Union. At the time of the crisis, America was the world's only nuclear power. This meant that the Soviets didn't shoot at US planes during the Airlift because they feared that America would respond with atomic weapons. This may have contributed to Stalin's desire for the USSR to develop its own nuclear bomb, which it did in 1949. America's nuclear advantage during the Airlift may have, therefore, contributed to rising tensions and competition between the two powers.

- Cold War tensions increased when Stalin had to end the blockade. He was forced to do this because the West's Airlift had been a success, and it had become clear that the West would not withdraw from Berlin. This raised tensions because the West had stopped Stalin from achieving his aim of driving them from the city.
- The Berlin Crisis was a massive propaganda victory for the USA, which made tensions between the two powers grow. The Airlift made America seem strong and it was seen as the defender of freedom against Soviet aggression. On the other hand, the failure of the blockade meant that Stalin was humiliated and discredited. He also faced criticism for the suffering the blockade had caused to West Berliners. This gave America the upper hand in the Cold War, which increased tension with the USSR.
- The Berlin Crisis increased Cold War tensions because it resulted in the formal division of Germany into West Germany, controlled by the USA and its allies, and East Germany, controlled by the communist USSR. This increased Cold War tensions by highlighting the division between the USA and the USSR, and between the capitalist and communist areas of Europe.

4 This question is level marked. How to grade your answer:

Level 1 1-4 marks	The answer gives a basic explanation of at least one factor. It presents a basic argument which has some structure. It shows limited relevant background knowledge.
Level 2 5-8 marks	The answer gives a simple explanation of at least one factor. It presents a simple argument which is organised and clearly relevant to the question. It shows some relevant background knowledge.
Level 3 9-12 marks	The answer gives a more developed explanation of the factor in the question and at least one other factor. It presents a developed argument which is well organised and directly relevant to the question. It shows a range of accurate and relevant background knowledge.
Level 4 13-16 marks	The answer gives a highly developed explanation of the factor in the question and at least one other factor, and reaches a well-supported judgement about the importance of those factors. It presents a complex and coherent argument which is organised in a highly logical way and fully focused on the question. It shows a range of accurate and detailed background knowledge that is relevant to the question.

Here are some points your answer may include:

- Stalin's desire to expand Soviet influence was a very important reason for the development of the Cold War between 1945 and 1949, because it led to rising tensions between the Soviet Union and the West. Before the Yalta Conference took place, Stalin had installed a pro-Soviet communist government in Poland. This concerned the Western powers, and at Yalta, Stalin promised to let non-communists join the Polish government and to hold free elections. However, by the time the Potsdam Conference took place around five months later, Stalin was installing a government in Poland made up solely of pro-communist members. This made Britain and the USA feel that Stalin had gone back on the promises he had made at Yalta. This led to rising tensions between the powers, which shows how Stalin's attempts to expand Soviet influence in Eastern Europe contributed to the progression of the Cold War.
- As the Soviet Union expanded its influence, a divide emerged in Europe between the communist East and capitalist West. This was an important development of the Cold War because it created two opposing sides in Europe and contributed to the breakdown of the Grand Alliance. Between 1945 and 1948, the Soviet Union installed puppet governments in Eastern European countries such as Romania, Hungary and Czechoslovakia in order to gain control over the region. Churchill referred to this split between East and West as the 'Iron Curtain', which made it clear that Britain and the USA now saw the USSR as a threat rather than an ally.
- The USSR's attempt to expand its influence by bringing the whole of Berlin under its control was a significant factor in the development of the Cold War. The USSR's effort to drive the Western powers out of the city by cutting off access to West Berlin was seen as hostile by the West, and they feared that the USSR might try to invade West Germany next. As a result, the Western powers began an Airlift to try to overcome the blockade. This was the first confrontation between the USSR and the USA, so it was a significant event in the development of the Cold War and was a direct result of Stalin's desire to expand Soviet influence.
- However, another important reason for the development of the Cold War was the USA's introduction of the Truman Doctrine and the Marshall Plan in 1947, which worsened relations and deepened divisions between East and West. The Truman Doctrine, which aimed to contain communism, made Stalin feel threatened. He also felt threatened by the Marshall Plan because he viewed it as a way for the USA to gain influence in Europe and spread capitalism. As a result, Stalin felt he had to react by strengthening his alliances in Eastern Europe through the creation of Cominform and Comecon. This helped strengthen the divisions between East and West in Europe, but Stalin was only acting in response to the Truman Doctrine and the Marshall Plan, which highlights America's role in the development of the Cold War.
- The USA's development and use of nuclear weapons was another important reason for the progression of the Cold War between 1945 and 1949. America had kept the details of its nuclear programme a secret from the Soviet Union, so when the USA dropped atom bombs on Hiroshima and Nagasaki in 1945, Stalin became more suspicious of the West. America's atomic weapons made the USSR feel threatened and increased the rivalry between the two countries, prompting Stalin to speed up the development of the Soviets' own atom bomb. This was the beginning of the arms race, an important factor in the development of the Cold War.
- American actions in Berlin between 1945 and 1949

Answers

also contributed to rising Cold War tensions. By 1948, the Western powers had united their zones in Berlin, established a single government there and introduced a new currency. As Berlin was in Soviet-occupied East Germany, it meant that this united Western zone was on the USSR's doorstep, which greatly alarmed Stalin. Furthermore, West Berlin was thriving, and this undermined communism and threatened the Soviet Union's authority. This contributed to Stalin's decision to begin the Berlin blockade, which shows the role the USA had in provoking this aggressive response.

- Overall, it was growing suspicion between the East and the West between 1945 and 1949 that led to the development of the Cold War. Stalin feared invasion from the West, so he wanted a sphere of influence in Eastern Europe to help protect the USSR. However, the growth of Soviet influence in Eastern Europe concerned the West, who believed that the USSR was attempting to aggressively spread communism at the expense of capitalism. The West then behaved in ways that threatened the USSR, which led the USSR to respond by tightening its hold over its sphere of influence. Therefore, suspicion between the superpowers led them both to act in ways that seemed aggressive and threatening to the other, and this led to the development of the Cold War.

The Development of the Cold War
Page 19 — The USSR and China
Knowledge and Understanding

1. Mao Tse-tung and his communist forces in China challenged the country's Nationalist government, led by Chiang Kai-shek. Chiang's government was corrupt and becoming increasingly unpopular. In contrast, the communists wanted to modernise the country and had a lot of support. This state of civil war continued for almost 25 years, until 1949 when the communists won the war. On 1st October 1949, Mao announced the creation of the People's Republic of China, and the Nationalist leaders fled to Taiwan.

2. • The USSR agreed to give China a loan of $300 million.
   • The two countries agreed that Soviet experts would be sent to China to help modernise the country.
   • The two countries agreed to defend each other if they were attacked by Japan or any country associated with Japan.

3. NSC-68 was a National Security Council Paper that claimed the Soviet Union planned to gain control over both Europe and Asia. It recommended that the USA should take a more aggressive approach to defending non-communist countries against the communist threat. As a result of this, the USA expanded its military and its nuclear weaponry.

Source Analysis

1. • In the cartoon, the USSR is shown as a man standing on top of the globe with his cape covering half the world. The countries on his cape are countries allied with the Soviet Union. This is critical of the USSR's foreign policy because it suggests that the USSR is like a conqueror who wants to spread communism across the world by adding more countries to his cape.
   • The cartoon shows half the globe covered in shadow by the USSR's long cape. This is critical of the USSR's attempts to increase its influence by suggesting that

communism is like a dark shadow that brings evil to the world.

2. • Source A is useful because it shows that by 1951, when the source was produced, it was an American belief that China was under the USSR's influence. In the cartoon, the USSR is shown as a conqueror, and the countries on its cape represent areas of Soviet influence. The cape contains the satellite states in Eastern Europe, but also includes China. This could be a reference to the alliance that had been developing between the USSR and China since 1949. In June 1949, Mao announced that he wanted China to become an ally of the USSR, and in February 1950 the two countries signed a treaty of friendship. Therefore, Source A is useful because it shows that in 1951, people in America believed that China had become a Soviet satellite state like the countries in Eastern Europe.
   • The usefulness of Source A is limited because it was produced by an American cartoonist, so it gives a one-sided view of the USSR's actions in Asia. The cartoon expresses American fears about the USSR's alliance with China that were often exaggerated. The USA felt threatened by the USSR's friendship with China and thought that the USSR was co-ordinating an international communist movement. Therefore, in the cartoon, the USSR is presented as a conqueror who has taken control of China and wants to continue expanding his control. In fact, far from 'conquering' China, Stalin wasn't involved in China becoming communist, and was actually hesitant to make an alliance with it.

3. • Source B is useful because it shows the US government's attitude towards the USSR's actions in Asia. Source B comes from NSC-68, which was completed in April 1950, two months after the USSR and China signed a treaty of friendship. NSC-68 was a government report that warned that the USSR was planning to dominate both Europe and Asia. This is shown in Source B, which argues that the USSR is aiming for 'the domination of the Eurasian land mass'. Therefore, the source is useful in showing American concerns that the Soviet alliance with China was the first step in the USSR's plan to gain control over both Europe and Asia.
   • The usefulness of Source B is limited because it was produced by the US government, so it is likely to express a one-sided and highly critical attitude towards the USSR's actions in Asia. The source was produced in April 1950, when the USA felt threatened because the USSR had just signed a treaty of friendship with China, and the USA feared that communism would continue to spread throughout Asia. This led Truman to take a tougher approach to containing the spread of communism by implementing NSC-68. Therefore, because Source B is an extract from NSC-68, it is likely to reflect this tougher attitude. This means that the source presents a critical and potentially exaggerated account of the USSR's actions in Asia.

Page 21 — Korea and Vietnam
Knowledge and Understanding

1. After the Second World War, Korea was divided. Soviet forces occupied the North and US forces occupied the South. Attempts to reunify the country failed as both the USA and the USSR promoted their political ideologies in each region, and two separate governments were set up in 1948. War broke out in June 1950 when Stalin agreed to

Answers

support an invasion of South Korea by North Korea, and provide their leader, Kim Il-sung, with weapons.

2   South Korea turned to the UN Security Council for help after it was invaded, and the USA proposed that the UN should support them. The USSR was not present at the meeting, since it had stopped attending Council meetings to protest the UN's refusal to recognise communist China. This meant that the USSR could not veto the proposal, so the proposal was passed and UN forces entered the war.

3   The Korean War ended in a stalemate and both sides agreed to a truce in 1953, meaning that North Korea remained communist and South Korea stayed non-communist.

4 a) Where two nations indirectly fight against one another by supporting opposite sides of a conflict.

   b) A French colony in Asia that included Vietnam.

   c) A group of rebels who opposed French rule in Vietnam, led by the communist, Ho Chi Minh.

   d) The belief that if Vietnam 'fell' to communism, then other countries in Southeast Asia would follow and the whole region would come under the influence of the USSR.

   e) A communist force in South Vietnam that was backed by the North. It aimed to overthrow Ngo Dinh Diem, an anti-communist leader put in charge of South Vietnam by the USA.

5   • 1940s — The Viet Minh, led by Ho Chi Minh, gain influence in Vietnam.
- 1950 — In January, the USSR and China recognise Ho Chi Minh as the legitimate leader of Vietnam.
- 1954 — The French are defeated by the Viet Minh in May, despite American aid being sent to help them. It is then decided that Vietnam will be temporarily split into communist North Vietnam and non-communist South Vietnam.
- 1955 — The USA helps to install Ngo Dinh Diem, an anti-communist leader, in South Vietnam.
- 1963 — Diem is overthrown and assassinated by his own military.
- 1965 — The first US combat troops are sent to Vietnam.
- 1968 — Over 500,000 US troops are in Vietnam.
- 1973 — The US withdraws its troops without victory.
- 1975 — Vietnam becomes a united, communist country.

Thinking Historically

1   Actions taken by the USA:
- The USA implemented NSC-68 and expanded its military and nuclear weaponry after the USSR signed a treaty of friendship with China. NSC-68 also recommended that the USA should take a more aggressive approach to defending non-communist countries in Asia against the Soviet threat.
- The USA promoted its ideology in South Korea and backed the anti-communist leader, Syngman Rhee.
- The USA proposed that the UN should support South Korea in the Korean War. US soldiers were sent to South Korea as part of UN forces, which were led by US general Douglas MacArthur.
- The USA sent aid to the French in Vietnam to help them resist the communist Viet Minh.
- The USA helped to install the anti-communist leader, Ngo Dinh Diem, in South Vietnam in 1955.
- The USA increased their involvement in Vietnam after Diem was overthrown. From 1965, US combat troops were sent to Vietnam, and by 1968 there were over 500,000 American troops there.

Actions taken by the USSR:
- The USSR recognised Mao as the rightful leader of China and supported communism in the country.
- The USSR signed a treaty of friendship with China in February 1950. They gave China a loan of $300 million, sent experts and advisors to help modernise China, and agreed to defend China if it was attacked by Japan or a country associated with Japan, such as the USA.
- The USSR stopped attending UN Security Council meetings to protest the UN's refusal to recognise communist China.
- The USSR promoted its ideology in North Korea and backed Kim Il-sung, the leader of communist North Korea.
- The USSR agreed to support an invasion of South Korea by North Korea, and provide North Korea with weapons for the invasion.
- The USSR supported North Korea against the UN forces in the Korean War by providing them with aircraft, tanks and artillery.
- The USSR recognised Ho Chi Minh as the legitimate leader of Vietnam in January 1950.
- The USSR supported North Vietnam and the Vietcong during the Vietnam War. The Soviets provided them with weapons such as missiles and radar systems.

2   You can choose either option, as long as you explain your answer. For example:
- The main reason for Cold War tensions in Asia was the actions taken by the USA. Although the USSR signed a treaty of friendship with China in 1950, the Soviets had little involvement in China becoming a communist country, and Stalin was hesitant to embrace China as an ally. The USSR's actions in China only increased tensions because the USA reacted so aggressively by implementing NSC-68. Similarly, although both countries contributed to tension in the Korean War by backing opposite sides, the USA was arguably most responsible for increasing tensions over Vietnam by sending troops there to fight against the Vietcong.
- The main reason for Cold War tensions in Asia was the actions taken by the USSR. The USA only became involved in Asia because the USSR supported the spread of communism there. For example, the USSR signed a treaty of friendship with China, and that forced the USA to take a tougher stance, implementing NSC-68 to tackle the threat of a Soviet stronghold developing in Asia. The USSR was also directly responsible for the conflict in Korea by supporting North Korea's invasion of South Korea in 1950 and providing the North Koreans with weapons. The actions of the USSR in China and Korea meant that the USA was worried about the spread of communism in Vietnam, leading to conflict between the two countries there.

Page 23 — Military Rivalries

Knowledge and Understanding

1   An arms race is when countries compete with each other to develop more powerful and more dangerous weapons than the other side.

2   The USA had used atomic bombs in Japan in 1945. Possession of such a powerful weapon gave the USA an advantage over the USSR, so the USSR wanted to develop nuclear weapons to compete with the USA and to defend their national security.

3 a) 1945 — The USA used atomic bombs in Japan. It was the

only country in the world that had nuclear weapons.

b) 1949 — The USSR succeeded in creating its own atom bomb.

c) 1952 — The USA detonated the first hydrogen bomb, which was around 500 times more powerful than the bombs dropped on Japan in 1945.

d) 1955 — The USSR developed its own powerful design of hydrogen bomb.

e) 1957 — In August, the Soviets successfully tested the first Intercontinental Ballistic Missile. It could strike the USA after being launched from the USSR.

f) 1959 — The USA's first successful ICBM test took place.

g) 1960 — The USA deployed submarines carrying Polaris missiles that could be fired from anywhere under the sea. These submarines were difficult to detect.

4 a) The formation of NATO in 1949 meant that the USSR felt vulnerable to attack.

b) The treaty of friendship led to fears in the West that the USSR was planning to spread communism throughout Asia and beyond.

Thinking Historically

1 The arms race worsened relations between the USA and the USSR because it heightened feelings of fear and suspicion between the two countries. Both sides were worried that the other would try to trigger a war if they gained a military advantage, so an intense rivalry developed as each country tried to develop more powerful weapons. However, the arms race also helped to reduce the threat of physical conflict between the powers. This was because of the threat of mutually assured destruction. Both the USA and the USSR had large numbers of nuclear weapons that could destroy each other. This meant that the two sides were reluctant to push each other into war because they wanted to avoid using such powerful weapons that could cause so much destruction.

Page 25 — Military Rivalries

Source Analysis

1 a) The USA sitting on top of Western European countries as they sign the treaty makes it seem as though the USA is forcing the Western European countries to become members of NATO. This suggests that the USA created NATO by controlling and dominating other countries. This is critical of NATO because it suggests that it is an unequal alliance controlled by the USA.

b) This suggests that the USA used its nuclear superiority to pressure European countries in to becoming members of NATO. This is critical of NATO because it suggests that the organisation is only held together by fear and intimidation. It is also critical of the organisation because it suggests that it is led by an aggressive and dangerous country who could potentially use nuclear weapons at any time.

2 The sources have different opinions because they were made by people from different sides of the Cold War and have different purposes. Source A is a Soviet cartoon, so it is likely to express a critical view of NATO because the Soviets felt threatened by the military alliance of western countries. This means that the source's purpose is to promote the view that NATO is an unpleasant and dangerous organisation. On the other hand, Source B is a speech by an American politician. This means that it is more likely to give a positive view of NATO and a negative view of the Warsaw Pact because the USA was a founding member of NATO and wanted to spread the idea that NATO was a stronger alliance than the Warsaw Pact.

3 The sources might be useful as a pair because they show the different attitudes that people on each side of the Cold War had towards NATO. Source A shows the Soviet attitude towards NATO, whereas Source B reflects the opinion of American politicians. Therefore, the two sources highlight the differences in perspective on either side of the Cold War, which helps to demonstrate why there was so much tension between the two sides.

Knowledge and Understanding

1 • October 1957 — The USSR launch Sputnik, the first satellite to be sent into space.
   • January 1958 — The USA launches its own satellite, called Explorer 1.
   • July 1958 — President Eisenhower founds the National Aeronautics and Space Administration (NASA) to focus on space research and exploration.
   • April 1961 — Yuri Gagarin of the USSR becomes the first person to travel into space.
   • May 1961 — Alan Shepard becomes the first American to go into space. President Kennedy claims the USA will put a man on the Moon by the end of the decade.
   • Early 1960s — The US government increases NASA's annual budget from $500 million to $5.2 billion. NASA begins to make plans for Project Apollo, a mission to the Moon.
   • 1969 — Apollo 11 is successful. Neil Armstrong and Buzz Aldrin become the first men to walk on the Moon.

2 Success in the space race was important because it became linked to power and status. The superpower that was ahead in the space race would seem more technologically advanced and might therefore be seen by the world as the superior power. For example, when the USSR was ahead in the space race early on, the USA worried that this would make people think communism was superior to capitalism.

3 The space race intensified the arms race, because the rockets used to launch satellites could also be used to carry ICBMs. Therefore, the launch of Sputnik in the USSR made it clear to the USA that the USSR would also be able to reach America with nuclear weapons. This meant that the USA's fears of a nuclear attack increased and the USA sped up its weapons programme.

Page 27 — The 'Thaw'

Knowledge and Understanding

1 • Many of the prisoners who were jailed under Stalin were released.
   • The death penalty was abolished.
   • The powers of Stalin's secret police were limited.
   • Statues of Stalin were taken down.

2 a) Stalin believed that war between capitalist and communist countries was inevitable, but Khrushchev believed in the idea of 'peaceful co-existence'. He thought that capitalist and communist countries could exist together without coming into conflict.

b) Stalin wanted tight control of countries in the Eastern Bloc. On the other hand, Khrushchev wanted to give them more political and economic freedom because he thought this would stabilise the communist regimes there.

3 Khrushchev continued to develop weapons, showing that he wanted the USSR to remain competitive with the USA.

4 Communism caused economic hardship in Eastern Europe, and poor living conditions made people resent the USSR.

Thinking Historically

1 a) Eisenhower became leader of the USA in January 1953

Answers

and Khrushchev became leader of the USSR in September 1953. With new leaders in charge of each country, there was a chance for a fresh start in relations.

b) The USA and USSR met in Geneva in 1955 and agreed to communicate more openly. In 1955, the USSR officially recognised West Germany as a state. This showed that the two sides could compromise and make agreements, which reduced tensions between them.

c) Khrushchev followed a policy of de-Stalinisation, which was popular with the USA, as they disliked Stalin's style of rule. Khrushchev's policy of 'peaceful co-existence' also reduced tension between the superpowers, since it created hope that they could live alongside each other without the need for conflict.

2 a) States in Eastern Europe begin to have more political and economic freedom from the USSR when Khrushchev abolishes Stalin's Cominform. Tensions in the satellite states rise to the surface because not all states had chosen communism. Some of them see a chance to loosen ties with the USSR.

b) The USSR threatens to intervene, but eventually allows the new government to follow their own version of communism. This encourages other states, such as Hungary, to consider revolt.

Page 29 — Hungary and the U2 Crisis
Thinking Historically

1 a) Rákosi's authoritarian regime becomes increasingly unpopular. In July 1956 he is removed from power and replaced with Erno Gero.

b) In October 1956, mass protests break out in Budapest.

c) Nagy announces a program of reforms. He plans to dissolve the secret police, review wages and pensions, and make sure that Soviet troops withdraw from Hungary. In November 1956, he announces that Hungary will withdraw from the Warsaw Pact and hold free elections.

2 a) Relations between the East and the West worsened as many in the West were shocked by the USSR's use of violence against the Hungarian people. The West thought that the invasion undermined 'peaceful co-existence' because it showed that the USSR could still be aggressive and would use violence to protect communism. However, relations between the East and the West didn't break down completely. This is because the West was afraid of interfering with the USSR's satellite states in case it started a nuclear war. The USA attempted to take action by holding a vote in the UN about the USSR's withdrawal from Hungary, but the USSR vetoed the vote. After this, the West took no further action against the USSR.

b) The invasion strengthened Soviet authority in Eastern Europe because it showed the satellite states that attempts to rebel against Soviet control would be met with force.

3   The U2 crisis caused a disagreement between the USA and the USSR over the issue of spying. The USSR shot down an American spy plane over Soviet territory, but the Americans denied they had been spying. The Soviets then produced the pilot and the plane's wreckage as proof. Although the USA eventually admitted to spying, Eisenhower still refused to apologise, arguing that the USA needed to use spy planes to protect itself against attacks. This behaviour worsened relations, leading Khrushchev to walk out of the 1960 Paris Peace Summit and cancel a trip Eisenhower was due to take to the USSR the following month. This worsened relations further because it meant that an opportunity for the two countries to work together

to discuss important issues, such as controls on nuclear weapon testing and the situation in Berlin had been lost.

Source Analysis

1 a) The source is from a speech made by President Eisenhower. This makes it useful for the investigation, because it shows how the American president at the time of the U2 crisis viewed the incident. However, this also means that the source gives a very one-sided view of the crisis, because we don't hear about Khrushchev's perspective as leader of the USSR.

b) The purpose of the speech is to defend the USA's use of a spy plane to collect information about the USSR. This makes it useful for the investigation because it shows how the US government justified their use of spying. However, as Eisenhower is trying to deflect blame away from the USA, he may be exaggerating the threat that the USSR posed to the USA.

c) The speech was made on 11th May 1960, ten days after the U2 plane was shot down. This makes it useful for the investigation because it shows how the USA responded to the incident shortly after it happened, and we can see that this response would have contributed to worsening relations. Eisenhower's response would have caused further tension with the Soviet Union because he criticises the USSR for its 'fetish of secrecy and concealment' and argues that this was a 'major cause of international tension and uneasiness'.

d) The content of the source is useful because it shows that the US government was not sorry for spying on the USSR because it believed that spying was necessary for the security of America. Eisenhower hints that the USSR is 'capable of massive surprise attack' and that the USA needs to spy on the USSR to protect the 'safety of the whole free world'. This is useful because it shows why the USA thought it needed U2 spy planes to collect information about the USSR.

Pages 32-33 — Exam-Style Questions

1   This question is level marked. How to grade your answer:

Level 1 1-2 marks	The answer gives a basic analysis of relevant features of the source's content and/or provenance. It is supported by simple background knowledge.
Level 2 3-4 marks	The answer gives a more developed analysis of relevant features of the source's content and/or provenance. It is supported by relevant background knowledge.

Here are some points your answer may include:

- We know that the poster supports the USSR's achievements in the space race because it emphasises Soviet successes. The poster portrays Yuri Gagarin and a rocket with the date 1961, together with the caption 'Long live Soviet man — the first cosmonaut!'. This is clearly celebrating Gagarin's mission in April 1961, when he became the first person to travel into space. By saying that Gagarin was the 'first cosmonaut', the caption is highlighting that his success was unprecedented and that the USSR had achieved something that no-one else, including America, had yet managed to do.

- We can also tell that the poster supports the USSR's achievements in the space race because it is a propaganda poster designed to highlight the Soviet Union's scientific expertise. This is because, at the time the poster was made, both the USA and the USSR were trying to outdo each other's achievements in space so that

Answers

they would be seen as the superior power. Therefore, this poster is publicising the USSR's achievements in the space race to try to make the USSR seem better than the USA. This is reflected in the poster's caption, which states 'Long live Soviet science!' to emphasise the success of science in the USSR.

2 This question is level marked. How to grade your answer:

Level 1 1-3 marks	The answer shows a limited understanding of one or both sources and gives a basic analysis of them.
Level 2 4-6 marks	The answer gives a simple evaluation of one or both sources based on their content and/or provenance.
Level 3 7-9 marks	The answer evaluates the content and/or provenance of both sources in more detail to make judgements about their usefulness.
Level 4 10-12 marks	The answer evaluates the content and provenance of both sources to make a developed judgement about their usefulness. The answer is supported with relevant background knowledge.

Here are some points your answer may include:

- Source B is useful because it shows how America believed that communism could spread throughout Asia. When Eisenhower made these comments, the communist Viet Minh were fighting the French for control of Vietnam, an area of Indochina. Eisenhower compares countries in Asia to a row of dominoes, stating that if Indochina 'falls' to communism then other countries, such as Japan and the Philippines, would follow until the whole area becomes communist. The source is useful, therefore, because it shows that America believed that communism could grow in Asia and that Vietnam was key to this expansion.

- Source B is useful because it shows that the spread of communism in Asia made America feel threatened. Eisenhower says that the loss of Asia would be 'incalculable to the free world', which suggests that he believed the spread of communism would negatively affect all democratic countries. He also states that Asia had already 'lost' 450 million people to 'the Communist dictatorship', and that the USA 'can't afford greater losses'. This could be referring to China becoming communist in 1949, and suggests that America believed it would be harmed by the further spread of communism in Asia. This is useful because it shows that the spread of communism in Asia made the USA feel vulnerable, which explains why the USA gave France aid to help them fight the Viet Minh, and why they became more heavily involved in Vietnam once France was defeated.

- Source C is useful because it shows that Americans believed communism was a dangerous and destructive force which had been spread into Asia by the Soviet Union. The source shows communism as a bird of prey dripping in blood, hovering over symbols of death and pain, such as bones and blood. This echoes the poster's caption that communism causes 'terrorism and assassination'. The source also features the hammer and sickle, a symbol of the Soviet Union, which reflects the fact that America believed that the Soviets were spreading their ideology in Asia as part of a global communist revolution.

- Source C is useful because it illustrates the fact that America didn't want communism to spread in Asia. The source is a piece of American propaganda, designed to spread anti-communist views. As it was published in South Vietnam following the split of the country, its purpose was probably to encourage people living there not to embrace communism. This highlights the USA's desire for Vietnam to resist becoming a fully communist country, and America's commitment to containing communism in Asia.

- Taken together, the sources are useful because they demonstrate the USA's concerns as communism spread in Asia. In the time between these two sources being produced, the situation in Vietnam had become much worse from a US perspective. Source B originates from April 1954, just before the French were defeated by the communist Viet Minh in May. Source C was created after the French had been defeated and Vietnam had been split into the communist North and the non-communist South. Therefore, these sources are useful when taken together because they reflect America's fear that communism would spread from Vietnam throughout Asia, and its concerns as communism became stronger in Vietnam.

- The usefulness of both sources is limited because they are American, and therefore only offer a Western perspective on the spread of communism in Asia. America had long been opposed to communism, believing that it was a danger to democracy and a threat to American power and influence. Both sources reflect this view. Source B directly expresses Eisenhower's beliefs, and Source C was produced by an agency established by Eisenhower, which means that it also portrays the view of the US government. While both sources make bold claims about the impact and extent of the spread of communism in Asia, these proved to be unfounded. Although Vietnam did 'fall' to communism in 1975, Southeast Asia didn't become a communist region.

3 This question is level marked. How to grade your answer:

Level 1 1-2 marks	The answer gives a basic analysis of causes and/or consequences. It lacks any clear organisation and shows limited relevant background knowledge.
Level 2 3-4 marks	The answer gives a simple analysis of causes and/or consequences. It has some organisation and it shows some relevant background knowledge.
Level 3 5-6 marks	The answer gives a more developed analysis of causes and/or consequences. It is well organised and shows a range of accurate and relevant background knowledge.
Level 4 7-8 marks	The answer gives a highly developed analysis of causes and/or consequences. It is very well organised and demonstrates a range of accurate and detailed background knowledge that is relevant to the question.

Here are some points your answer may include:

- The arms race increased tensions between the Soviet Union and the USA because the creation of such a dangerous weapon as the atom bomb made both powers feel threatened by each other. America's possession of the atom bomb, which it used against Japan in 1945, meant that it had an advantage over the USSR. This made the USSR feel threatened, particularly as Cold War tensions began to escalate. This led the USSR to develop its own atom bomb, which it succeeded in doing in 1949. This meant that America now felt threatened by the USSR, which caused tensions between them to rise.

- The arms race increased tensions between the USSR and

Answers

the USA by developing into an intense rivalry between the superpowers. Both powers feared that if the other had a nuclear advantage, they may be tempted to begin a war. This led both countries to develop more and more powerful and dangerous weapons. For example, in 1952, America developed the hydrogen bomb. Not wanting to fall behind, the Soviet Union created its own hydrogen bomb in 1955. Similarly, when the Soviets tested the first Intercontinental Ballistic Missile (ICBM) in 1957, the USA worked to develop its own. This constant competition and determination to stop the other power gaining a nuclear advantage meant that tensions between America and the Soviet Union grew.

- The arms race caused tensions between the powers to escalate by increasing the threat that the powers posed to one another. The creation of ever more dangerous weapons made both powers increasingly scared and suspicious of each other because they feared the devastation that these weapons could cause. The hydrogen bomb that America exploded in 1952 was 500 times more powerful than the bombs they had dropped in Japan in 1945. The Soviet development of ICBMs in 1957 meant that the scale of the arms race escalated even further. These weapons were capable of reaching the USA after being launched from within the USSR, and were practically unstoppable. Therefore, as the arms race developed, so did the capabilities of nuclear weapons. This helped to increase tensions between the superpowers because they were worried what the consequences would be if either side used their weapons.

- Another way the arms race increased tensions between America and the Soviets was when the two powers responded to other events during the Cold War by building up their nuclear weapons. For example, when the Soviets felt threatened by the formation of NATO in 1949, they increased their efforts to develop nuclear weapons. When China 'fell' to communism in 1949 and later signed a treaty of friendship with the Soviet Union, the USA felt vulnerable because they believed that this proved communism was a growing threat. As a result, America responded by increasing its nuclear and military weaponry through NSC-68. This shows how nuclear weapons became a response to other escalating Cold War tensions, but the development and stockpiling of these weapons only served to further increase tensions between the Soviet Union and the USA.

4   This question is level marked. How to grade your answer:

Level 1 1-4 marks	The answer gives a basic explanation of at least one factor. It presents a basic argument which has some structure. It shows limited relevant background knowledge.
Level 2 5-8 marks	The answer gives a simple explanation of at least one factor. It presents a simple argument which is organised and clearly relevant to the question. It shows some relevant background knowledge.
Level 3 9-12 marks	The answer gives a more developed explanation of the factor in the question and at least one other factor. It presents a developed argument which is well organised and directly relevant to the question. It shows a range of accurate and relevant background knowledge.
Level 4 13-16 marks	The answer gives a highly developed explanation of the factor in the question and at least one other factor, and reaches a well-supported judgement about the importance of those factors. It presents a complex and coherent argument which is organised in a highly logical way and fully focused on the question. It shows a range of accurate and detailed background knowledge that is relevant to the question.

Here are some points your answer may include:

- The Hungarian Uprising contributed to worsening relations between the East and the West because it helped to reignite tensions between the two superpowers at a time when relations seemed to be improving. When Khrushchev became leader of the USSR in 1953, he spoke of 'peaceful co-existence' with the West and it seemed as though tensions between America and the Soviet Union might 'thaw'. However, Khrushchev's decision to invade Hungary to preserve Soviet influence there showed that the USSR would continue to use aggression to maintain its sphere of influence. This invasion undermined peaceful co-existence, and showed that there was still a definite divide between the USSR and the West.

- The Hungarian Uprising also damaged East-West relations because it demonstrated the lengths the Soviet Union would go to in order to maintain its power in Eastern Europe. In its attempt to keep Hungary under its control, the USSR sent tanks into the country. Thousands of Hungarians were killed or injured, and the Hungarian leader, Imre Nagy, was arrested and hanged. The USSR's brutality against the Hungarians shocked the West. Also, the Soviet Union's decision to veto a United Nations vote on whether it should withdraw from Hungary highlighted its reluctance to co-operate with the West, and caused relations between the superpowers to worsen.

- Although the Hungarian Uprising undermined peaceful co-existence, there were limits to how far relations deteriorated over this event. The Western powers condemned the USSR's actions in Hungary and took the issue to the United Nations, but they took no further action on the matter when the Soviets vetoed the UN vote. They were reluctant to interfere in the Soviet satellite states, because they feared this might cause a nuclear war to break out. Therefore, the Hungarian Uprising showed that the West believed it necessary to avoid increasing tensions with the Soviets over a country that was already in their sphere of influence.

- The U2 crisis also played an important part in undermining 'peaceful co-existence' and worsening relations between the East and West. When the USSR shot down an American spy plane over Soviet territory in 1960, Eisenhower initially denied that it was a spy plane, then after he admitted the truth, he refused to apologise to the USSR. This led to heightened distrust between the powers. It also resulted in Khrushchev abandoning the Paris Peace Summit a few days later, where the superpowers had planned to discuss key issues, such as tensions in Berlin and nuclear weapons testing. Khrushchev also called off a trip Eisenhower had been due to take to the USSR. The cancellation of these events, which may have improved relations between the superpowers, meant that tensions increased, and the relationship between the East and the West suffered.

- The most important reason for worsening relations between 1950 and 1960 was the spread of communism into Asia. During the Hungarian Uprising, the USSR acted in an existing Soviet satellite state. However, the threat that Asian countries may begin to come under Soviet influence alarmed the West more because it seemed as though communism was spreading throughout the rest of the world, and this greatly damaged East-West relations. In 1949, China had become a communist nation, and in 1950, its leader, Mao Tse-tung, signed a treaty of friendship with the USSR. This led the USA to fear that Stalin was directing a worldwide communist revolution. As a result, America implemented NSC-68, which saw the USA increase its nuclear and military weaponry, and adopt a more aggressive approach to what it saw as the Soviet threat. This shows that the USA's concern over the spread of communism significantly harmed relations between the two superpowers.
- The growth of communism in Asia caused both powers to become involved in conflicts in the region, and this led to the further deterioration of East-West relations. During the Korean War, Stalin provided support for Kim Il-sung (the North Korean communist leader) and his invasion of the non-communist South. The USA encouraged the UN to protect the South, and provided many troops to fight on the UN's behalf, as well as a US general, Douglas MacArthur, to lead the troops. As a result, the Korean War became a proxy war, where America and the Soviet Union supported opposite sides of the conflict, without actually going to war with one another. Therefore, this conflict allowed both powers to act out wider Cold War tensions, which caused East-West relations to deteriorate.
- Asia was also the source of worsening relations when it seemed that communism was spreading to Vietnam. America was worried that the growing influence of communism in Vietnam was proof that Soviet-backed communism was spreading. This made the USA more suspicious of the USSR. As a result, America tried to contain communism in Vietnam by supporting the French troops fighting the Viet Minh, and then becoming more heavily involved after France's defeat in 1954 by supporting non-communists in the South. This heightened distrust and rivalry between the powers, which damaged East-West relations.

Transformation of the Cold War
Page 35 — The Berlin Question
Knowledge and Understanding
1 a) The movement of large numbers of people from East Berlin to West Berlin in the years after the Berlin crisis.
   b) The demand issued by Khrushchev in 1958 that all US, British and French troops leave West Berlin within six months, allowing West Berlin to become a free city.
2 West Berlin's economy developed quickly after it became a unified zone in 1948, benefitting from a new currency and aid received from the American Marshall Plan. In contrast, the USSR had drained East Berlin of resources and it suffered from slow economic development. In addition, many skilled workers left East Berlin during the refugee crisis, making it even more difficult for East Berlin's economy to develop.
3 a) • The USSR felt threatened by the economic success of capitalist West Berlin.

- The USSR was worried about the fact that East Berlin's economy relied on trade links with West Berlin.
- The USSR was concerned that the West was deliberately using West Berlin's strong economy to interfere in Eastern Europe.
- Khrushchev was embarrassed by the large numbers of refugees leaving East Berlin to go to West Berlin, because it suggested that they preferred life under capitalism to life under communism.
   b) • The West began to see West Berlin as a symbol of democracy that needed to be protected.
- The refugee crisis was good propaganda for the West, because large numbers of refugees leaving East Berlin made communism look weak.
4 Khrushchev became the first communist leader to visit the USA, symbolising a new spirit of communication between the superpowers. Although the leaders didn't reach an agreement over Berlin, the summit seemed positive because they decided to meet again in Paris the following year to discuss the matter further.

Thinking Historically
1 a) Khrushchev issued the Berlin Ultimatum in 1958, demanding that all US, British and French troops leave West Berlin within six months.
   b) Eisenhower refused the ultimatum.
   c) West Berlin had become a symbol of democracy after the Berlin Airlift, so the West felt it had to continue to support the city. Eisenhower couldn't agree to the ultimatum because if the USA abandoned West Berlin, it would lose credibility as a supporter of democracy.
   d) The situation in Berlin stayed unresolved and continued to be a point of tension between the West and the USSR.
2 • The USA refused to apologise for the U2 incident, causing Khrushchev to walk out of the Paris Peace Summit in May 1960. This meant that the two countries were less likely to come to an agreement about Berlin because relations between them had soured and there was no opportunity for Eisenhower and Khrushchev to discuss the Berlin situation.
- Kennedy had replaced Eisenhower as president by the time the superpowers met again at Vienna in June 1961. Kennedy wanted to take a tougher approach towards communism than Eisenhower had, and promised to defend the rights of the USA in West Berlin. Both Kennedy and Khrushchev refused to compromise, so no resolution was reached.

Page 37 — The Berlin Wall
Knowledge and Understanding
1 The failure of the Vienna Summit led the USSR to believe that the problems in Berlin couldn't be solved by negotiation. As a result, Khrushchev decided to build the Berlin Wall to stop any more refugees leaving East Berlin.
2 At first, American troops and diplomats were allowed to cross into East Berlin after the wall was built. However, East German border guards began to restrict their entry. The Americans responded by moving tanks up to Checkpoint Charlie, where they were met by Soviet tanks. The stand-off between the two sides lasted for around 16 hours and it seemed as though war might be a possibility. However, neither side wanted to risk conflict and they both agreed to withdraw their tanks after Kennedy contacted Khrushchev.

Answers

Source Analysis

1 a) The author of the source is President Kennedy, leader of the USA. This makes the speech useful for the investigation because it shows America's official response to the construction of the Berlin Wall.

   b) Kennedy's speech was made in 1963, two years after the Berlin Wall was constructed. This makes it useful for investigating the USA's long-term response to the construction of the Berlin Wall, although it is less useful for investigating the immediate response.

   c) The purpose of the source is to publicly criticise communism and the Berlin Wall. This makes it useful for the investigation because it shows that the USA responded to the construction of the Berlin Wall by using it for anti-communist propaganda. However, the fact that this source is propaganda also limits its usefulness because it means that Kennedy is unlikely to discuss the fact that he was also relieved by the building of the Berlin Wall. Therefore, the source doesn't give a full picture of the USA's response to the wall.

   d) The content of the source makes it useful for the investigation because it shows how the USA criticised the construction of the Berlin Wall. Kennedy describes the wall as 'an offense against humanity' and claims that it is 'dividing a people who wish to be joined together'. This demonstrates how the USA argued that the USSR was oppressing the people of Germany. Kennedy also claims that the Berlin Wall highlights 'the failures of the Communist system', demonstrating how the USA used the Berlin Wall for anti-communist propaganda.

Thinking Historically

1 a) The construction of the Berlin Wall gave the USA the chance to spread anti-communist propaganda. The Americans argued that the wall showed communism was failing because the only way the USSR could stop people leaving East Germany was to build a wall. They wanted people to see the wall as a symbol of oppression, and they argued that West Berlin represented freedom in the struggle against communism.

   b) The construction of the Berlin Wall restricted movement between East and West Berlin, meaning that East Berliners could no longer work in West Berlin. Friends and families who lived on opposite sides of the wall were separated from each other, and those who tried to escape from East Berlin were shot. However, the construction of the wall also put an end to the huge numbers of people leaving East Berlin. This benefitted East Germans, as it meant that their country had the chance to rebuild its economy and to strengthen itself as a communist state.

   c) In East Germany, the wall was often called the 'Anti-fascist Protective Rampart', with the East German government claiming that the wall was necessary to keep out western spies and protect East Germany.

2 The construction of the Berlin Wall helped to avoid open conflict between the superpowers. The wall allowed Khrushchev to try to strengthen East Germany as a communist state, and although Kennedy condemned the wall, he was also relieved by it because he saw it as evidence that the USSR wasn't going to try to take West Berlin by force. Despite this, the Berlin Wall became a symbol of the divide between East and West in the Cold War and showed that there was still a lot of tension between the superpowers.

Page 39 — The Cuban Missile Crisis

Knowledge and Understanding

1 Under Batista's rule, people in Cuba lived in a ruthless military dictatorship. Most people lived in poverty, while American businessmen and the Mafia made huge profits.

2 Castro began a guerilla war against Batista in 1956. By 1959, he had enough support to capture Havana and managed to overthrow the government.

3 Importance to the USA:
   • The USA had a long economic history with Cuba. The USA held most of the shares in Cuban industry and owned half of Cuba's land.
   • The USA wanted Cuba to be non-communist. The USA felt threatened by the possibility of a communist state emerging on its doorstep, and it wanted to prevent the spread of communism from Cuba to Latin America.

   Importance to the USSR:
   • Castro was sympathetic towards communism, so he made a useful ally.
   • Cuba was very close to US soil, so was a useful place for the USSR to gain influence.

Thinking Historically

1 a) After Castro became leader, he seemed to move towards communism. He nationalised industries and increased taxes on goods imported from America. This caused concern for the USA.

   b) Castro signed a trade agreement with the USSR, who promised to buy all of Cuba's sugar exports. He also confiscated all remaining US property in Cuba.

2 You can answer either way, as long as you explain your answer. For example:
   This action was not the most important reason why Cuba and the USSR developed a closer relationship. Although the USA's intervention accidentally pushed Castro closer to the USSR, he was already sympathetic to communism. It is therefore likely that he would have strengthened Cuba's ties with the USSR anyway, even without intervention from the USA.

3 Kennedy didn't want the USA to have a communist neighbour on its doorstep and he feared that communism might spread through Latin America to countries like Brazil, Bolivia and Venezuela. Therefore, he acted on advice from military advisors and authorised the Bay of Pigs invasion by anti-Castro rebels to try to remove Castro.

4 • The USA was humiliated by the failure of the invasion.
   • Cuba was pushed even closer to the USSR and Castro announced that he was a communist in December 1961.
   • Tensions continued to grow between Cuba and the USA.
   • Castro decided Cuba needed military assistance from the USSR, which led to the Cuban Missile Crisis.

Page 41 — The Cuban Missile Crisis

Knowledge and Understanding

1 • 1952 — Batista established his dictatorship in Cuba.
   • 1956 — Castro began a guerilla war against Batista.
   • 1959 — Castro took over Havana and overthrew Batista's government. He nationalised US companies in Cuba and increased taxes on imported US goods.
   • January 1961 — The USA severed all diplomatic ties with Cuba, and Kennedy no longer recognised Castro's government.
   • April 1961 — Anti-Castro rebels backed by the USA attempted to invade Cuba. They were easily defeated at

Answers

the Bay of Pigs.

- September 1961 — Cuba asked the USSR for weapons to defend itself against US intervention.
- December 1961 — Castro publicly announced that he was a communist.
- April 1962 — The USA placed nuclear missiles in Turkey, right next to the USSR.
- July 1962 — Khrushchev decided to put missiles in Cuba.
- October 1962 — US spy planes spotted missile bases being built in Cuba. Kennedy demanded that Khrushchev dismantle the bases, and he ordered a naval blockade of Cuba. The USA sent bombers into the air carrying nuclear weapons and prepared to invade Cuba. Eventually, the USSR made a deal to dismantle the bases and turn its ships around, in return for the secret removal of US missiles from Turkey.

Thinking Historically

1 a) • Soviet missiles were removed from Cuba.
- Kennedy was seen as a hero for standing up to communism.
- Khrushchev was humiliated and resigned in 1964.

b) • The USA had been humiliated at the Bay of Pigs.
- US missiles were removed from Turkey.
- Cuba remained communist and the USA promised not to invade.

2 a) A telephone hotline was established between Washington and Moscow in 1963 so that the USA and the USSR could talk quickly and directly in a crisis.

b) • The Limited Test Ban Treaty was signed in 1963. It stated that all future nuclear weapons tests had to be carried out underground to avoid radiation polluting the air.
- The Outer Space Treaty was created in 1967. It prevented any countries from placing weapons of mass destruction in space.
- The Nuclear Non-Proliferation Treaty came into force in 1970. Both superpowers agreed that they wouldn't supply nuclear weapons to countries that didn't already have them, to try to stop nuclear weapons from spreading. This treaty also encouraged nuclear disarmament, but allowed the use of nuclear technology for peaceful purposes, such as supplying energy.

Source Analysis

1 • The source is useful because it shows how the USSR's actions in Cuba helped to cause the Cuban Missile Crisis. In the source, Kennedy describes the 'build-up of Communist missiles' in Cuba as 'deliberately provocative' and 'unjustified'. Therefore, the source is useful because it shows that the USSR's decision to build military bases in Cuba led to the Cuban Missile Crisis by causing outrage in the USA and forcing Kennedy to take action. Kennedy did this by blockading Cuba, putting bombers carrying nuclear bombs into the air and preparing for an invasion of Cuba.
- The source is useful because it shows how the USA contributed to the Cuban Missile Crisis. Kennedy says that the USSR's actions 'cannot be accepted by this country', which implies that the USA will act against the USSR. Indeed, Kennedy ordered a naval blockade of Cuba to try to prevent missiles being taken there the same day the source was produced. The source, therefore, is from the time that the USA was responding to Soviet actions in Cuba, which makes it useful for showing the USA's role in escalating the tension between the two superpowers.

- The usefulness of the source is limited because it gives a one-sided view of the causes of the Cuban Missile Crisis by portraying the USSR as the aggressor and the USA as an innocent victim. The source comes from a public speech by Kennedy, who, as leader of the USA, would have wanted to portray the USSR negatively and the USA positively. For example, in his speech, Kennedy claims that US 'missiles have never been transferred to the territory of any other nation'. In fact, the USA had placed missiles in Turkey, right next to the USSR, in April 1962. This suggests that Kennedy is distorting the truth in his speech because he wants the USA to be seen as the victim of Soviet aggression, rather than also being responsible for causing the crisis.

Page 43 — The Prague Spring
Knowledge and Understanding

1 Czechoslovakia and the USSR had close political and economic ties before 1968. The USSR had made Czechoslovakia one of its communist satellite states in 1948, meaning that Czechoslovakia's policies had been heavily influenced by the USSR. As a member of the Warsaw Pact, Czechoslovakia was expected to only trade within the Eastern Bloc and to follow Soviet-style communism. However, there had been growing discontent about Soviet control over Czechoslovakia, including protests in 1956.

2 The Prague Spring was a four month period in 1968 when reforms introduced by Dubcek were tolerated by the USSR, and Czechoslovakia experienced relative freedom from Soviet control.

3 • Dubcek reopened the border with West Germany.
- People were now allowed to travel freely to the West.
- He decentralised all industry, taking control of Czechoslovakian companies away from Communist Party officials and giving more power to local authorities.
- Trade unions and workers were given more power.
- The reforms introduced freedom of speech and allowed the creation of opposition parties in politics.

4 Dubcek wanted to improve Czechoslovakia's economy by moving away from Soviet policies that had slowed the country's economic progress, such as collectivisation and centralisation. Soviet policies that restricted free speech and freedom of movement were unpopular in Czechoslovakia, so Dubcek's reforms addressed these issues too.

5 Dubcek promised that Czechoslovakia would still be a loyal ally to the USSR and that it would remain a member of the Warsaw Pact.

Thinking Historically

1 a) Dubcek's reforms had weakened the USSR's control over Czechoslovakia, and Brezhnev was concerned that if the country was allowed to pull any further away from Soviet control, other parts of the Eastern Bloc would follow suit. By intervening in Czechoslovakia, he hoped to send a message to the rest of the Eastern Bloc that they would not be allowed to break away from the USSR.

b) In August 1968, President Tito of Yugoslavia visited Prague. Despite leading a communist country in Eastern Europe, President Tito had refused to sign the Warsaw Pact and had never accepted the USSR's version of communism. His visit heightened Brezhnev's fears that Czechoslovakia was no longer loyal to the USSR and encouraged him to intervene in order to prevent Dubcek withdrawing even further from Soviet control.

Answers

c) Czechoslovakian communists sent the USSR a letter in August 1968 asking for help. This gave Brezhnev a reason to intervene in Czechoslovakia.

Source Analysis

1 a) The content of the source is useful because it shows that people in Britain supported Dubcek carrying out reform in Czechoslovakia, but that they had doubts over the future of the Prague Spring. In the cartoon, the vine emerging from Stalin's grave and wrapping around Dubcek seems threatening and dangerous, which suggests that the USSR might destroy Dubcek's reforms. The reforms that Dubcek introduced, such as allowing opposition parties, went against Soviet-style communism. Dubcek is holding scissors and looks as though he is about to cut the vine, which suggests that people in Britain believed that Dubcek needed to completely cut off links to the USSR or else the Prague Spring would not be successful.

b) The cartoon was produced in July 1968, during the Prague Spring. Dubcek had introduced his reforms in April 1968, so the source is useful because it shows how people in Britain responded to Dubcek's reforms shortly after they were introduced. It shows that people recognised only a couple of months after Dubcek introduced his reforms that the USSR may restrict his actions.

c) The source was produced in Britain, and this limits its usefulness. It gives a good indication of Western attitudes towards the Prague Spring, and suggests that members of the British public were supportive of Dubcek's efforts to distance Czechoslovakia from the USSR's influence. However, the source only gives a one-sided representation of attitudes towards the Prague Spring because it doesn't depict attitudes in the East or in Czechoslovakia itself.

Page 45 — The Prague Spring

Knowledge and Understanding

1 a) 500,000 Soviet troops invaded Czechoslovakia on 21st August 1968.

b) The Czechoslovakians responded with non-violent demonstrations, and one student burned himself alive in protest in January 1969. They responded in this way because they were keen to avoid a repeat of the violence that had occurred during the Hungarian Uprising in 1956.

c) In April 1969, Dubcek was replaced by Gustav Husak, who followed Soviet-style communism and would keep Czechoslovakia loyal to the USSR.

2 a) Western countries condemned the Soviet action but didn't intervene because they were worried about interfering with the USSR's sphere of influence. The West was also wary about taking action because the Cold War had thawed slightly and nobody wanted to re-ignite tensions. President Lyndon B. Johnson cancelled a summit meeting with Brezhnev in response to the USSR's actions.

b) The UN denounced the invasion and proposed a draft resolution requesting the withdrawal of Soviet troops from Czechoslovakia. However, this was vetoed by the USSR.

c) Communist parties in the West criticised Brezhnev's reaction and tried to distance themselves from Soviet influence.

d) Some of the Eastern Bloc countries disagreed with the USSR's actions, and relations with the USSR worsened as a result. Romania and Albania both refused to participate in the invasion. Albania withdrew from the Warsaw Pact shortly afterwards.

3 The Brezhnev Doctrine was an announcement made by Brezhnev after the invasion of Czechoslovakia that the USSR would act to protect communism in any country where it was under threat.

Source Analysis

1 a) The source comes from a speech made by Brezhnev. This makes it useful for the investigation because it shows the USSR's official attitude to the invasion of Czechoslovakia and the reasons why it believed an invasion was necessary.

b) The purpose of the speech is to defend the USSR's decision to intervene in Czechoslovakia. This makes the source useful for the investigation, because it shows how the USSR justified the invasion. For example, Brezhnev explains that Czechoslovakia becoming independent would have been 'detrimental to the other socialist states'. However, the usefulness of the source is limited because it doesn't mention how the invasion was also an attempt to protect the power and influence of the USSR. Brezhnev would not have wanted to highlight these more selfish interests in a speech designed to justify the invasion.

c) The speech was made in November 1968, a few months after Soviet troops invaded Czechoslovakia, when protests in the country were still ongoing. This makes the source useful for the investigation because it shows how the USSR responded to the invasion at a time when the Soviet government was facing criticism from other countries and from the people of Czechoslovakia.

d) In the source, Brezhnev explains that the USSR can't allow the 'weakening' of socialism in any of its satellite states, and that Dubcek's reforms would have been 'detrimental to the other socialist states'. This makes the source useful for the investigation because it shows that the USSR believed the invasion of Czechoslovakia was justified because it was necessary to protect communism and the countries of Eastern Europe.

2 • The content of Source B makes it useful because it shows that people in Britain protested against the invasion of Czechoslovakia. In the photograph, people are holding up banners that say 'Free Czechoslovakia' and 'Halt Soviet Imperialism'. This suggests that some people in the West strongly disagreed with the invasion of Czechoslovakia and wanted Western countries to take action against the USSR.

• The photograph was taken in August 1968, in the same month that the Soviet troops invaded Czechoslovakia. This makes it useful for the investigation because it shows that there was opposition in the West to the invasion shortly after it took place.

3 The sources are useful as a pair because they show how attitudes to the invasion were different in the USSR and the West. Source A shows that the USSR thought the invasion was necessary to protect communism, while Source B shows that people in the West viewed the invasion as an unnecessary act of aggression. This helps to explain why there was tension between the USSR and the West over the invasion.

Page 47 — Détente

Knowledge and Understanding

1 A period in the 1970s when tensions between the USA and the USSR eased, and relations between the two superpowers improved.

2 There was tension over the issue of human rights. The USA criticised the USSR for denying citizens religious and political freedoms, as well as freedom of speech and the right to emigrate. Tension was also caused by America's increasing involvement in Vietnam and the USSR's

intervention in Czechoslovakia.

3 a) Nixon needed a foreign policy success to draw attention away from criticism he was facing at home for the Vietnam War.

b) Brezhnev was worried by a visit Nixon made to China in February 1972. He wanted to make sure that China and the USA wouldn't join forces against the USSR.

4 ABMs are anti-ballistic missiles. They were designed to intercept and destroy incoming missiles. They threatened to upset the nuclear balance because if one side had ABMs and the other didn't, the side with ABMs could launch a first strike and then just destroy the missiles that were fired back towards them. This meant that the threat of retaliation would be gone.

5 a) Its aim was to slow down the arms race and ease tensions.

b) The two sides agreed to limit the number of ABMs that each of them could have. They also agreed to a temporary limit on the number of ICBMs on both sides.

c) The treaty reduced the likelihood of one country holding an advantage over the other, since the number of ABMs a country could have was limited.

Thinking Historically

1 • Point — The crisis in Berlin in the 1960s convinced both superpowers that a new strategy was needed to reduce tensions between them.

• Evidence — Kennedy and Khrushchev were both unwilling to compromise over Berlin when they met in 1961. The USSR built the Berlin Wall later in the same year. Conflict nearly broke out between them at Checkpoint Charlie because of this.

• Why evidence supports point — The Berlin question and conflict at Checkpoint Charlie showed that a refusal to compromise on both sides increased tensions and made conflict more likely. The two superpowers didn't want to risk war, so they realised the importance of a period of détente in the 1970s to reduce tensions.

• Point — Although the crises in the 1960s were important in encouraging the superpowers to improve relations, the financial problems that both countries faced by the 1970s were a more important reason why there was a period of détente.

• Evidence — In the 1970s, both sides were struggling financially. The US economy was suffering from rising inflation and the cost of the Vietnam War, and the USSR was concerned with falling living standards in Eastern Europe. The arms race was very expensive for both sides.

• Why evidence supports point — Both superpowers had financial problems and couldn't afford to keep funding the arms race, so they saw the advantage of reducing their military spending and increasing trade with each other. This meant that they were keen to reduce tensions and so there was a period of détente. The fact that there was a reduction of tension in the 1970s rather than the 1960s suggests that the superpowers' financial problems played a more important role in causing a period of détente than the crises in the 1960s.

• Point — Another important reason for the period of détente was the changing relationship between China and the two superpowers by the 1970s.

• Evidence — China was becoming more powerful by the 1970s, and its alliance with the USSR had weakened. In contrast, the USA had improved its relations with China, and Nixon visited China in February 1972.

• Why evidence supports point — There was a period of détente in the 1970s because the USSR wanted to avoid the possibility of the USA and China forming an alliance against it. This made the USSR more open to co-operating with the USA than they had been in the 1960s, even when crises like the Cuban Missile Crisis had brought the two superpowers close to war.

Pages 50-51 — Exam-Style Questions

1 This question is level marked. How to grade your answer:

Level 1
1-2 marks — The answer gives a basic analysis of relevant features of the source's content and/or provenance. It is supported by simple background knowledge.

Level 2
3-4 marks — The answer gives a more developed analysis of relevant features of the source's content and/or provenance. It is supported by relevant background knowledge.

Here are some points your answer may include:

• We know that Source A is critical of the Soviet Union because it suggests that Soviet control of East Berlin has caused the economy to suffer. The half of the man's body in East Berlin is wearing shabby clothes, as his trousers are torn and his shoes have holes in them. This suggests that people living in East Berlin were poor, which reflects the fact that the USSR drained East Berlin of resources after it took control of the area after the Second World War. In contrast, the clothes on the half of the man's body in West Berlin are smart and in good condition. This represents the prosperity of West Berlin, which developed economically under the control of the Western powers, benefitting from a new currency and Marshall Plan aid. Therefore, we can tell that the cartoon is critical of the Soviet Union because it is showing East Berlin to be inferior to West Berlin.

• We know that Source A is critical of the Soviet Union because it shows that the Berlin Wall had a harsh impact on the people of Berlin. The man in the cartoon seems to be trapped by the wall, one half of his body separated from the other. This reflects the fact that the wall was constructed overnight on 13th August 1961, instantly dividing East Berlin and West Berlin. Berliners were not allowed to cross the wall, which meant that they were separated from friends and family. East Berliners could no longer work in West Berlin, and anyone who tried to escape East Berlin was shot. The depiction of the man as trapped shows that the source is critical of Khrushchev's decision to build the wall and trap people in either the East or the West.

• Source A was drawn by a Hungarian artist who spent time in a Soviet prison camp in the 1940s. This makes it more likely that he has a critical attitude towards the USSR, and might want to draw attention to how the actions of the Soviet Union have caused people to suffer.

2 This question is level marked. How to grade your answer:

Level 1
1-3 marks — The answer shows a limited understanding of one or both sources and gives a basic analysis of them.

Level 2
4-6 marks — The answer gives a simple evaluation of one or both sources based on their content and/or provenance.

Level 3
7-9 marks — The answer evaluates the content and/or provenance of both sources in more detail to make judgements about their usefulness.

68

Answers

Level 4
10-12 marks

The answer evaluates the content and provenance of both sources to make a developed judgement about their usefulness. The answer is supported with relevant background knowledge.

Here are some points your answer may include:

- Source B is useful because it shows that some communists believed that America was responsible for the Bay of Pigs invasion. President Kennedy had tried to hide the USA's involvement in this attempt to overthrow Castro's communist regime in April 1961. However, the cartoon, created by the communist artist Herluf Bidstrup, depicts the USA reaching to stab Cuba with a knife, revealing that some communists clearly blamed America for the invasion. The source also seems to suggest that the USA's invasion was unjustified because Cuba is presented as doing nothing to deserve such a violent and aggressive attack. Bidstrup's violent depiction of the USA's actions in this cartoon, therefore, shows that the invasion was viewed by some communists as an American-led, unprovoked attack on Cuba.

- Source B is useful because it shows that some communists thought that the USSR should defend Cuba against the aggression that the USA showed in its Bay of Pigs invasion. In the cartoon, the USSR is shown grabbing hold of the USA's arm as it stabs Cuba. This shows that communists believed that a strong and forceful response was needed against the USA's attempt to invade. The USSR is shown as a strong and powerful arm determined to stop the USA, while America is depicted as a dark and wicked figure. This suggests that communists saw the USSR as a force for good, working against the evil influence of America.

- Source C is useful because it shows that the Soviet government was critical of the USA and Kennedy for the Bay of Pigs invasion. This can be seen in the language that Khrushchev uses, when he describes the American invasion as a 'gangster attack' and an example of 'armed aggression'. This shows that Khrushchev viewed America's actions in Cuba as aggressive and hostile. The source also shows that Khrushchev believed that the USA was unjustified in carrying out the Bay of Pigs invasion. He refers to 'the lawful Government and people of Cuba', which shows that he believed that the Cuban government was legitimate and so it should not be overthrown by the USA. Therefore, the source is useful because it shows that the USSR was critical of what it saw as the USA's aggressive and unjustified actions at the Bay of Pigs.

- Source C comes from a letter written by the leader of the USSR, Nikita Khrushchev, on 22nd April, shortly after the Bay of Pigs invasion began on 17th April. Therefore, the source is useful because it gives a direct insight into Khrushchev's attitude towards Cuba around the time of the invasion and how he interacted with Kennedy over the attack. Khrushchev's critical attitude towards the USA's actions and the way he communicates this to Kennedy shows how the Bay of Pigs invasion caused tension between the superpowers.

- Taken together, the sources are useful because they show that the Soviet government and other communists thought that the USA was acting aggressively during the Bay of Pigs invasion, and that the attack was unprovoked and unjustified. Therefore, these sources reveal attitudes that provide an insight into why the USSR decided to

help Castro when he asked them for military support after the Bay of Pigs invasion.

- The usefulness of both sources is limited because they only provide a view of pro-Soviet attitudes towards the Bay of Pigs invasion. Neither source provides insight into American attitudes and what motivated Kennedy to authorise the attack. The USA was worried that Cuba was moving towards communism and that it was creating ties with the USSR, after Castro nationalised US companies in 1959 and later signed a trade agreement with the USSR. Kennedy felt threatened by the possibility of a communist state on the USA's doorstep, and he was afraid that communism could spread from Cuba across Latin America. However, American concerns about the spread of communism are not reflected in either of the sources, which both portray the USA's actions at the Bay of Pigs as aggressive and unjustified.

3   This question is level marked. How to grade your answer:

Level 1
1-2 marks

The answer gives a basic analysis of causes and/or consequences. It lacks any clear organisation and shows limited relevant background knowledge.

Level 2
3-4 marks

The answer gives a simple analysis of causes and/or consequences. It has some organisation and it shows some relevant background knowledge.

Level 3
5-6 marks

The answer gives a more developed analysis of causes and/or consequences. It is well organised and shows a range of accurate and relevant background knowledge.

Level 4
7-8 marks

The answer gives a highly developed analysis of causes and/or consequences. It is very well organised and demonstrates a range of accurate and detailed background knowledge that is relevant to the question.

Here are some points your answer may include:

- The USSR's invasion of Czechoslovakia caused international tensions by showing that there were still serious divisions between the Soviet Union and the West. At a time when East-West tensions had thawed slightly, the invasion showed the West that the USSR was still determined to preserve its sphere of influence by any means necessary and maintain a strong anti-Western alliance. This caused tensions by highlighting the rivalry that still existed between the East and the West.

- The West reacted to the invasion by condemning the USSR, which shows how the USSR's actions strained relations. President Johnson also cancelled a scheduled meeting with Brezhnev, which reflects how the invasion led to a worsening of relations between the two powers.

- The invasion caused international tensions by showing the West that the USSR was unwilling to co-operate with them. After the Soviets invaded Czechoslovakia, the UN condemned their actions, and when the UN asked the USSR to withdraw their forces from Czechoslovakia, the Soviets vetoed this request. This caused international tensions, as it showed the West that the Soviet Union wouldn't participate in diplomacy with them.

- The USSR's invasion of Czechoslovakia caused international tensions because it strained the relationship between the USSR and some of its satellite states. Some countries within the Eastern Bloc felt threatened by the USSR's reaction in Czechoslovakia and the force that Soviet troops had used. Romania and Albania had refused to assist the USSR in the invasion, and Albania even withdrew from the Warsaw Pact shortly afterwards. The Soviets' behaviour also caused a deep resentment to develop between Czechoslovakia and the USSR. This shows that even the USSR's closest allies felt threatened and shocked by the invasion, and it severely damaged their relations with the Soviet Union.

- International tensions increased further shortly after the invasion of Czechoslovakia, when the Soviet Union introduced the Brezhnev Doctrine. The Brezhnev Doctrine stated that the USSR would take action in any country where it felt that communism was under threat, and this caused concern in many communist nations. For example, China now feared that the Soviets would use the Brezhnev Doctrine to justify an invasion. The policy also caused concern in the West because it showed that it was now the USSR's official policy to continue to use force in order to maintain its power and influence. This caused tension by making it clear that the Cold War was set to continue.

4   This question is level marked. How to grade your answer:

Level 1 1-4 marks	The answer gives a basic explanation of at least one factor. It presents a basic argument which has some structure. It shows limited relevant background knowledge.
Level 2 5-8 marks	The answer gives a simple explanation of at least one factor. It presents a simple argument which is organised and clearly relevant to the question. It shows some relevant background knowledge.
Level 3 9-12 marks	The answer gives a more developed explanation of the factor in the question and at least one other factor. It presents a developed argument which is well organised and directly relevant to the question. It shows a range of accurate and relevant background knowledge.
Level 4 13-16 marks	The answer gives a highly developed explanation of the factor in the question and at least one other factor, and reaches a well-supported judgement about the importance of those factors. It presents a complex and coherent argument which is organised in a highly logical way and fully focused on the question. It shows a range of accurate and detailed background knowledge that is relevant to the question.

Here are some points your answer may include:

- The construction of the Berlin Wall in 1961 caused Cold War tensions because it demonstrated to the West that the USSR was willing to use aggression and cause suffering in order to preserve its sphere of influence. The Soviets constructed the Berlin Wall to try to strengthen East Berlin by stopping mass emigration to West Berlin. This attempt to protect communism in East Berlin restricted people's freedom, forcefully separated friends and families, and East Berliners who attempted to cross the wall were killed. This aggressive action from the USSR and the hardship it caused led the West to condemn the USSR, and increased tensions between them.
- The USA used the construction of the Berlin Wall as an anti-communist propaganda opportunity, and this caused Cold War tensions because the USSR would have seen this as an attack on communism. America argued that the wall was a symbol of oppression, and that the Soviets being forced to build a barrier to stop people

leaving communist East Berlin proved the superiority of capitalism. Kennedy also travelled to West Berlin in 1963 and made a speech where he stated that West Berlin represented freedom in the struggle against communism. These attempts by America to use the wall to discredit communism and portray the USSR as cruel would have caused Cold War tensions to grow.

- In addition to this, the construction of the Berlin Wall led to situations which brought the superpowers close to conflict. For example, after Soviet guards at the wall began denying US officials entry into East Berlin, a tense stand-off between American and Soviet tanks took place at Checkpoint Charlie in October 1961. This incident greatly increased tensions between the superpowers because it briefly seemed that war might break out.

- However, although the construction of the Berlin Wall caused some Cold War tensions, it also served to ease some of the tensions that had existed over Berlin. Tensions had emerged because West Berlin's thriving economy prompted skilled workers from the East of the city to move West, which humiliated the Soviets, as it suggested that living under capitalism was preferable to communism. However, the wall eased these tensions because it stopped workers leaving, meaning that East Berlin could try to rebuild its economy and strengthen itself. The building of the wall also relieved President Kennedy, because it reassured him that the Soviets didn't intend to occupy West Berlin or start a war over the city. As a result, some Cold War tensions decreased.

- There were other reasons for Cold War tensions in the 1960s. The USSR's invasion of Czechoslovakia caused tensions to rise because it was seen by the West as another aggressive Soviet attempt to maintain its sphere of influence. When the Czechoslovakian communist leader, Alexander Dubcek, introduced reforms which went against Soviet policy, the USSR felt threatened and ordered Soviet troops to invade the country in order to reassert its control. This showed the West that the USSR was prepared to use force to protect communism and preserve a strong anti-Western alliance. This caused tensions because it highlighted the divide between East and West, making it clear that the Cold War wasn't over.

- However, the most important source of tension between the superpowers in the 1960s was the Cuban Missile Crisis, as this developed into one of the most critical events of the Cold War. Cuba, an island off the coast of America, had become increasingly close with the Soviet Union, and Cuba's leader, Fidel Castro, officially announced that he was a communist in December 1961. This concerned the USA, as it brought the communist threat to America's doorstep. Tensions increased further in October 1962, when the USA discovered that the Soviets had placed missiles on Cuba. America refused to tolerate this, and escalated the situation by placing a naval blockade around the island and putting bombers carrying missiles into the air. The actions of both powers, therefore, pushed the world to the brink of nuclear war over Cuba. Although America and the Soviet Union seemed to come close to war over the incident at Checkpoint Charlie, the direct involvement of nuclear weapons made the Cuban Missile Crisis a much more tense and threatening situation.

Index

A

ABM (anti-ballistic missile) 46
Apollo missions 24
arms race 8, 22, 24, 46
atom bombs 8, 22
Attlee, Clement 6

B

Bay of Pigs 38
Berlin
  Airlift 12, 34
  crisis 12, 46
  Ultimatum 34
  Wall 36
Brezhnev Doctrine 44
Brezhnev, Leonid 42, 44, 46

C

capitalism 6, 10, 12, 26, 34
Castro, Fidel 38, 40
Checkpoint Charlie 36
China 18, 44, 46
Churchill, Winston 6, 8
Comecon 10
Cominform 10, 26
communism 6, 8, 10, 12, 18, 20,
  26, 28, 34, 38, 42, 44
containment 10, 18
Cuban Missile Crisis 38, 40, 46
Czechoslovakia 8, 42, 44

D

de-Stalinisation 26
détente 40, 46
domino theory 20
Dubcek, Alexander 42, 44

E

Eastern Bloc 24, 26, 42, 44, 46
Eisenhower, Dwight 26, 28,
  34, 38

F

Federal Republic of Germany
  12, 26

G

Gagarin, Yuri 24
German Democratic Republic 12
Grand Alliance 6

H

Ho Chi Minh 20
Hungarian Uprising 28, 44
hydrogen bombs 22

I

ICBM (Intercontinental Ballistic
  Missile) 22, 24, 46
Iron Curtain 8

K

Kennedy, John F. 24, 34, 36,
  38, 40
Khrushchev, Nikita 26, 28, 34,
  36, 38, 40
Korean War 20

L

Limited Test Ban Treaty 40

M

MAD (mutually assured destruction)
  22
Mao Tse-tung 18, 44
Marshall Plan 10, 34

N

Nagy, Imre 28
NASA (National Aeronautics and
  Space Administration) 24
NATO (North Atlantic Treaty
  Organisation) 22, 24
Nixon, Richard 46
NSC-68 18
Nuclear Non-Proliferation Treaty 40

O

Outer Space Treaty 40

P

Paris Peace Summit 28, 34
Peaceful co-existence 26
Poland 6, 8, 26
Polaris missiles 22
Potsdam Conference 6, 8, 12
Prague Spring 42, 44

R

Roosevelt, Franklin D. 6

S

SALT 1 (First Strategic Arms
  Limitation Treaty) 46
satellite states 8, 24, 26, 28
space race 24
Sputnik 24
Stalin, Joseph 6, 8, 10, 12, 18,
  20, 26

T

'Thaw', The 26
Tito 10, 42
treaty of friendship 18, 22
Truman Doctrine 10
Truman, Harry 6, 8, 10, 18

U

U2 crisis 28, 34
UN (United Nations) 6, 20, 28

V

Vienna Summit 34
Vietcong 20
Viet Minh 20
Vietnam War 20, 46

W

Warsaw Pact 24, 28, 42, 44

Y

Yalta Conference 6
Yugoslavia 10, 42

HAEWO41